HOW TO PLEASE GOD

DR. Y. BUR

AS IT PLEASES GOD® MOVEMENT

ASITPLEASESGOD.COM

HOW TO PLEASE GOD

Copyright © 2023 by Dr. Y. Bur. All rights reserved.

Visit www.RoarPublishingGroup.com for more information. No part of this publication may be reproduced, stored in a retrieval system, or transmitted in any way by any means, electronic, mechanical, photocopy, recording, or otherwise, without the prior permission of the author except as provided by USA copyright law.

Book design copyright © 2023 by R.O.A.R. International Group. All rights reserved.

R.O.A.R. Publishing Group
581 N. Park Ave. Ste. #725
Apopka, FL 32704
ROAR-58-2316
762-758-2316
www.RoarPublishingGroup.com
DrYBur@gmail.com

Published in the United States of America
ISBN: 978-1-948936-82-8
$22.88

Send *As It Pleases God* ®

Book Series **and** *Workbook* **Testimonies, Donations, Questions, or Orders to:**

Dr. Y. Bur
R.O.A.R. Publishing Group
581 N. Park Ave. Ste. #725
Apopka, FL 32704
ROAR-58-2316
762-758-2316
✉ Dr.YBur@gmail.com

Visit Us At:
📷 AsItPleasesGodMovement
AsItPleasesGod

🖥 DrYBur.com
🖥 AsItPleasesGod.com

Please Donate

Please DONATE to this *Missionable Movement of God* as a GIVE-BACK to the Kingdom. Thanks for your support. Many Blessings.

AIPG Donation Link

Scan to Pay

ASITPLEASESGOD.COM

Available Titles

ASITPLEASESGOD.COM

Table of Contents

Introduction	11
Chapter One	19
The Big Question	19
The Divine Reach	23
Salt of the Earth	24
Dealing with Judgment	28
Dealing with Assumptions	30
Remove the Plank	34
Chapter 2	43
Signature Effect	43
Gratefulness	46
Divine Favor	49
Kingdom Absolutes	51
The Portion	53
Chapter 3	55
Resonating Sound	55
What Displeases God?	58

  The Natural Elements 60
  Benefits of Pleasing God 65
  The Mastering Process 70
Chapter 4 77
 Spiritual Mirror 77
  Spiritually Investing 82
Chapter 5 93
 All ONE 93
  Divine Praying Power 96
  The Spiritual Team 102
  Spiritual Covering 106
  Under the Veil 110
  Using Pitch 112
  Spiritual Integrity 113
  Spiritually Alert 114
  Opt for the Lesson 117
Chapter 6 121
 Authenticity 121
  Divine Triggering 125
  It Is For You 126
  False Measures 126
  Keys to the Kingdom 128
  Spiritual Reshuffling 129
  Being You 132

Chapter 7 137
　Spiritual Interdependence 137
　　Self-Analysis... 139
　　Would You Know? 140
　　Enough is Enough 143
　　Reversing Mud Pies.. 145
　　Align or Misalign 149
　　Rock Solid.. 151
Chapter 8 153
　How To Please God 153
　　Pushing The Limit 156
　　The Seed 160
　　Dropping Our Nets.. 162
　　Spiritual Classroom.. 168
　　Spiritually Sharp 170
　　Dealing With Gaps... 172
　　Developing Our Conscience... 182
　　Overcoming Spiritual Error... 184
Chapter 9 191
　Divine Illumination 191
　　The Understanding 193
　　Morsel of Goodness 195
Chapter 10 197
　Spiritual Access.. 197

Paving the Way 200
Stay On Ready 202
Clipped Wings 207

Chapter 11 209
Growing Great 209
The Guarantee 211
Guarding The Tongue 214

Chapter 12 219
Spiritual Vetting 219
Playing Possum 222
The Promises of God 228
Age of Faith 234

INTRODUCTION

We all desire the Promises of God, but why are they seemingly held up or eluding us? Could it be that we are not surrendering to His Divine Will, Covenants, Authority, or Blueprint? Could it be that we are caught up in doing our own or the wrong things? Could it be that our negative mindsets are blocking us from maximizing our full potential? Then again, is it that we want God to bow down to us or please us on our own terms?

In any event, is it possible that we lack the understanding of His Divine Expectations, why He expects them from us, and how to properly ALIGN ourselves with His Promises, *As It Pleases Him*?

Now, *The Big Question* is, do we think the Divine Promises of God are NOT real, or do we think it is a fairytale from yesteryear? Are we secretly doubting Him or His Divine Potential? We can sit around laughing, doubting, pouting, criticizing, vetting, or rerouting, but *"God is not a man, that He should lie, nor a son of man, that He should repent. Has He said, and will He not do? Or has He spoken, and will He not make it good?"* Numbers 23:19.

The Promises of God are REAL, and if the Holy Spirit has not confirmed this from within, we have work to do. Why must we put in the work, especially when we are clueless about what we need to do and why? In the Eye of God, cluelessness is not an excuse to become lackadaisical in or out of the Kingdom.

Nor should we ever think that we can outsmart the Holy Trinity (The Father, Son, and Holy Spirit). Why can we not outsmart them, especially when having free will and a mind to think? Unfortunately, it increases our testing with fiery darts, targeting what we love or idolize the most. Or, it may cause us to become a plague in Earthen Vessels, targeting the psyche with soul ties, yokes, emptiness, and bondage that we have the propensity to lie about, whitewash, or deny. For the record, know this:

- ☐ No one knows everything.
- ☐ We are all clueless about something.
- ☐ We are all on a learning curve, publicly or privately.
- ☐ No one is 100% perfect.
- ☐ We all have room for growth.
- ☐ We are all a work-in-progress.
- ☐ We all have a Predestined Blueprint.
- ☐ We all have our types, likes, and dislikes.

If we DO NOT know who we are, our place in the Kingdom, or that we are Spiritual Beings first and foremost, we become overlooked by Spiritual Omission due to the lack of Spiritual Growth or outright Spiritual Error.

According to the Heavenly of Heavens, due to our Spiritual DNA, without the elements of growth in and out of the Kingdom, it becomes challenging to WIN in the Eye of God, even if we are in denial or appearing to win on our own terms.

Listen, if we are growing in the things of the world and NOT growing in the Kingdom, we create our own Spiritual Deficit by default, depriving ourselves of our Blueprinted Benefits and Divine Provisions.

How is it possible to deprive ourselves, especially when having it going on, needing nothing from no one? If we DO

NOT meet the Spiritual Contingencies, *As It Pleases God*, the Spiritual Veil must remain. It does not matter who we are, why we are, what we have, or what we do not have...the Spiritual Veil from the Heavenly of Heavens is REAL. Frankly, we DO NOT want to play around in this area with a flawed heart posture, a lack of humility, negative mindsets, continual rebellion, uncontrollable emotions, or loose lips.

The bottom line is that we choose our course in life through our free will, even if we have been PREDESTINED for a specific Mission. Here is the Spiritual Seal or Covenant we need to know, "*I call Heaven and Earth as witnesses today against you, that I have set before you life and death, blessing and cursing; therefore choose life, that both you and your descendants may live; that you may love the LORD your God, that you may obey His voice, and that you may cling to Him, for He is your life and the length of your days; and that you may dwell in the land which the LORD swore to your fathers, to Abraham, Isaac, and Jacob, to give them.*" Deuteronomy 30:19-20.

In the Promises of God, our Predestined Blueprint will NOT impede upon our self-made or self-willed plans. Why does He not force this on us? Firstly, we were not created as robots. Secondly, what God has for us, we have to WANT it, TILL for it, UNDERSTAND it, and POSITION ourselves accordingly, and *As It Pleases Him*. If not, we are in charge of creating the illusions appearing like promises OUTSIDE of the Promises of God, while our lives become a cycle of déjà vu until we come to ourselves.

On top of the repetitive cycles with various characters, Heaven and Earth become witnesses to our Seasons, Seeds, and Vicissitudes. At the same time, they do what it takes to get our attention, allowing the Winds, Storms, and Cycles of Life to shake us to the core. Or, they may even do a number on the human psyche to awaken the desire to seek help, pushing us out of our comfort zone and blocking us from certain Spiritual Gardens, similar to the Adam and Eve Experience.

What do Heaven and Earth have to do with anything, especially when we have the right to live our lives the way we desire? First and foremost, we did not create ourselves. Secondly, this is a God-Ruled Nation, even if it does not appear as such to the naked eye. Thirdly, we are all children of God, even if we fail to admit it or obey Him. Lastly, if everything in Heaven and on Earth obeys God, what makes us any different?

Then again, do we think we get a FREE PASS on forging our own treaties because we seemingly get away with our underlying debauchery? Meanwhile, the same debauched measures that are sown are the same ones designed with a more strategic plan to make us look like boo-boo the fool for undermining our Forefathers and trying to recreate a wheel that is already rolling. What does this mean in layman's terms? A wheel within a wheel becomes defeated by trying to outdo what is already there.

Simply put, a self-created battle cannot compare to a Spiritual Battle with a PROMISE hovering over it. And, just because we do not understand something does not make it unreal or untrue. Is this Biblical? I would have it no other way! *"Now as I looked at the living creatures, behold, a wheel was on the earth beside each living creature with its four faces. The appearance of the wheels and their workings was like the color of beryl, and all four had the same likeness. The appearance of their workings was, as it were, a wheel in the middle of a wheel. When they moved, they went toward any one of four directions; they did not turn aside when they went. As for their rims, they were so high they were awesome; and their rims were full of eyes, all around the four of them. When the living creatures went, the wheels went beside them; and when the living creatures were lifted up from the earth, the wheels were lifted up. Wherever the spirit wanted to go, they went, because there the spirit went; and the wheels were lifted together with them, for the spirit of the living creatures was in the wheels. When those went, these went; when those stood, these stood; and when those were lifted* up from the earth, the wheels were lifted up together with them, for the spirit of the living creatures was in the wheels." Ezekiel 1:15-21.

Unbeknown to most, DISOBEDIENCE contributed to the DNA hiccup within mankind in the first place. Therefore, if we do not WILLFULLY obey God, we cannot blame anyone or anything for our reality. Why must we assume responsibility? When we are disobedient, it does not begin or end with God; it is a manifestation leading to all manner of self-deficiency. How do we make this make sense? We overlook a human plague that cannot be seen with the naked eye until the damage is done from the inside out, even affecting the innocent until it is Spiritually Contained.

What does all of this have to do with the Promises of God? We are Spiritual Beings having a human experience in Earthen Vessels. If we fail to understand this fact, Divine Wisdom avoids us, and our Spiritual Blueprint lays dormant until we are ready. Furthermore, we become Spiritually Blind, Deaf, and Mute in Kingdom Formalities, heeding to the people, places, and things of our worldly system without restraint.

To add insult to injury, we fall into the trap of thinking everyone around us has issues without taking a second look in the mirror. Listen, if we fail to see ourselves clearly from God's Perspective or examine ourselves correctly while lacking humility and gratefulness, we commit Spiritual Purgatory upon ourselves without realizing it.

If we do not RESPECT who we are in Spirit and Truth, *As It Pleases God*, the Realm of the Spirit will not trust us with its Divine or Mysterious Secrets, Wisdom, and Powers. Why do we get deprived? Due to the probability of its selfish misuse. For example, this is similar to King Saul's abuse and misuse of power for selfish gain, popularity, brainwashing, and manipulative control.

Furthermore, King Saul secretly coveted and competed against God's Elect (The Prophet Samuel and King David). He also attempted to change the trajectory of God's Divine Will to fit his wants, needs, agendas, and desires. All of these are done to feed the lust of the eyes, the lust of the flesh, the pride of life, and to make God a liar just for power, money, sex, status, and fame.

Clearly, I am not here to point the finger, pass blame, or nitpick. I am here to Spiritually Guide us on properly using our hands in the Eye of God. What does this mean? I am Divinely Appointed to bring a Supernatural Awareness, giving the Spiritual Tools needed to help us become Kingdomly Mindful, *As It Pleases God.*

What is the purpose of becoming MINDFUL in such a manner? Frankly, we all have a little bit of this Saul Spirit running through our veins. Really? Yes, really! According to the Heavenly of Heavens, this plague (negative character traits) or Spirit of Saul (similar to the Spirit of Jezebel) must be Spiritually Contained, especially when God's Promises are involved.

Why must they be Spiritually Contained? They have destructive effects, invoking pride, anger, fear, insecurity, manipulation, disobedience, complaining, deceitfulness, unforgiveness, resentfulness, and rebellion against God, all in His Divine Name as a cover-up. Meanwhile, it leads innocent people away from God and to the slaughter. How so? By promoting the worship of false gods, engaging in immoral practices, causing division, and instigating chaos.

Regardless of how life appears to the naked eye, the inability to accept correction leads to pride, stubbornness, and arrogance. On the other hand, the refusal to submit to God's Divine Will in or out of the Kingdom is a recipe for disaster. Why would secret or open rebellion become a recipe for disaster? It comes with an internal yoke or stronghold of NEVER being satisfied with anything or anyone.

How can we avoid traveling down a destructive path of ungratefulness or dissatisfaction? We must develop a willingness to submit to the Will of God and our Predestined Blueprint, *As It Pleases Him*. They will help us AVOID the pitfalls associated with negative mindsets and rotten fruits that lead us and others away from Him or the Kingdom.

On the other hand, when we are willfully led toward the Kingdom of God, *As It Pleases Him*, it will come with a Spiritual Covering, protecting what belongs to Him. Thus, we must learn and understand how to walk the walk and talk the talk with a Spiritual Language from the Heavenly of Heavens.

Is it humanly possible to have a Spiritual Language or *Resounding Sound* reaching the Heavens Above? Absolutely! Once again, we are Spiritual Beings having a human experience...so, we must connect to God, *Spirit to Spirit*.

According to the Heavenly of Heavens, regardless of where we are from or what we are going through, we MUST become a positive work-in-progress, developing a Kingdom Mindset with a *Spiritual Mirror* to maximize our highest and greatest potential. Amid the intertwining or casting of the good, bad, or indifferent, we are responsible for extracting and converting them into lessons, understandings, and teachings through the Power of our Testimony without being on the take.

Why must we become a Living Testimony? Sharing Divine Knowledge and Practical Wisdom, *As It Pleases God*, with the correct motives, will cause all things to work together for our good with a *Resonating Sound* of GREATNESS. And with this book, we will share how to do likewise with GUARANTEED results, helping to avoid 'getting got' with the issues of life or what is unawaringly hidden within.

How can this book make such a guarantee? We do not make the guarantee personally out of selfishness or arrogance. The Holy Spirit uses Dr. Y. Bur as a Spiritual Vessel to convey the Word of God of Divine Relevancy, penetrating man's heart based on where they have been, where they are, and where they are going.

Unfortunately, this is not a one-and-done process but an ongoing *Spirit to Spirit* Relationship. How so? By placing people, places, and things into their proper perspective, obtaining the *Signature Effect* and Seals of the Kingdom, *As It Pleases God*, it causes Divine Revelation to find us, granting us what we need to go to the next level, with a *Spiritual Interdependency* trumping human reasoning.

Nevertheless, if one is content with where they are, then this book on *How To Please God* is NOT the cup of tea being sought. But if our Spiritual Gauge is ready to RECEIVE, thus saith the Lord from the Divine Negev of Living Water, this is the long-awaited Thirst Quencher of being *All One*.

If you are ready to become a Spiritual Ambassador for the Kingdom, *As It Pleases God*, let us go deeper to develop the *Spirit to Spirit* Connection together as ONE. As I extend my Spiritual Hand to you, *Spirit to Spirit*, let us take this long-awaited journey together as the *Voice of God* resonates, getting you on the right track while unfolding your Divine Blueprint.

www.DrYBur.com

CHAPTER ONE
THE BIG QUESTION

I n Earthen Vessels, we have come to *The Big Question* regarding *How To Please God* for real. According to the Heavenly of Heavens, the day of pretense is coming to a complete halt as we know it, with a Spiritual Demand and Seal of AUTHENTICITY.

Authentic or not, how do we *Please God* when our souls are crying out? Do we keep crying? Do we pick up the pieces and move on? Do we fight for what does or does not belong to us? Do we lie down, allowing life to happen? Do we try to make sense of it, do we go with the flow, or do we run and hide, waiting for something to happen? When our soul is wailing or buffering in ways we cannot articulate, who do we run to for help? If one has not asked or answered these questions, live a little longer. Life has a way of putting us to the test to determine what we are made of.

For our Heaven on Earth Experience, and as we live life in real-time with or without a Biblical Foundation, there are many things we can do in our own strength, not having to answer to anyone. On the other hand, there are some things in life that we need Divine Intervention or Accountability for God to intercede on our behalf, especially when desiring a *Signature Effect* or when becoming the Crème de la Crème.

When dealing with *The Big Question*, the *Resonating Sound* and our POWER are hidden in plain sight through our ability to know God, pray, repent, forgive, develop an understanding of all things, and utilize the Fruits of the Spirit. However, the truth is that we tend to expect others to do what we are unwilling or refuse to do for ourselves. Nor do we take the time to query ourselves, people, places, and things, *As It Pleases God*, while opting for self-pleasure, self-aggrandizement, and people-pleasing as our go-to.

Our lifestyle has a profound impact on the vitality of the questions we ask, answer, avoid, whitewash, or pander. If you are reading this book, it is time for you to forgive the impact that your cultural lifestyle may have had on you and move on in the Spirit of Excellence.

Why must we move on as Believers? In the Kingdom of God, positive growth, *As It Pleases Him*, is required. The eradication of being placed in a box or held back must be crushed right now. You are free to be who God created you to be with no shame attached. So, from this point forward, I need you to own your truth with a Positive Mental Attitude while bringing forth the desires of your heart. Nonetheless, when doing so, know this: *"Whoever does not carry his own cross and come after Me, cannot be My disciple."* Luke 14:27. For this reason, it is crucial to stop lying to yourself about yourself and start owning your truth and working on yourself, *As It Pleases God*!

Once you own your truth and become more positive in your way of thinking, questioning, and approaching, then I need you to trust God to open up your Destiny-Enriched Provisions to allow your GIFTS to make room for you.

Now, the best way I have found to put your faith into action is to create an action plan. It may take some time to document what you are seeing MENTALLY, but do not give up. If you can document every day, it will become easier for you to enact your Spiritual Mirror of reflection, making it easier to flow, download, and upload information, *Spirit to Spirit*.

When it comes down to *The Big Question*, we may be able to provide for our own daily needs physically. Nonetheless, in the Eye of God, we are required to push a little further than our physical needs, wants, and desires. As a matter of fact, I want to bring into question our Spiritual needs, our Emotional needs, our Mental needs, as well as our Spiritual Guidance.

With this *Spiritual Mirror*, I am going to need you to dig deep. Yes, dig deep within the depths of your soul to pull out any unconfessed or suppressed longings you need to uproot in order to REGRAFT the impact of your negative character traits. Why is this so important to do? You cannot fix or heal what you lie about, deny, or whitewash.

By all means, when willfully refusing to do our due diligence or self-correct, *As It Pleases God*, it is an atrocity to develop the nerve to blame someone else. How so? We point the finger for our mishaps, setbacks, selfishness, and atrocities in life, without using the *Spiritual Mirror* provided by our Heavenly Father to save, deliver, reform, and train us.

How do we know if we are NOT using our Spiritual Mirrors correctly? When we detach ourselves from our Spiritual Birthright or Inheritance, we will secretly or openly wallow in behaviors or characteristics, casting negative debris without realizing it. For our sake, we cannot leave our lives and the psyche AS-IS. Nor can we leave it secretly out of control, compounding the negative without elevating, overcoming, or doing something about it. Why? The way in which we are grafted Mentally, Physically, Emotionally, and Spiritually determines:

- ☐ Our DECISIONS.
- ☐ Our THOUGHTS.
- ☐ Our BELIEFS.
- ☐ Our sense of REASONING.
- ☐ Our INTELLECT.

- ☐ Our JUDGMENT.
- ☐ Our WILL.
- ☐ Our UNDERSTANDING.
- ☐ Our CONSCIENCE.
- ☐ Our CHARACTER.
- ☐ Our FRUITS.

Unfortunately, the *Spiritual Mirror* analysis will vary from person to person, situation to situation, trauma to trauma, culture to culture, and so on. However, here are the types of questions to ask yourself, but not limited to such:

- ☐ How do you react when you do not get what you want?
- ☐ Are you controlling your emotions, or are they getting the best of you?
- ☐ Can you control your tongue, or has your mouth become your greatest downfall?
- ☐ Are you lashing out or rejecting others out of spite?
- ☐ Is rudeness, unkindness, selfishness, or hatefulness plaguing your relationships?
- ☐ Does chaos and confusion have a bullseye on your life?
- ☐ Do you have a hard time staying committed to something or someone?
- ☐ Is negative mental chatter driving you insane or keeping you all over the place?

If we are honest with ourselves, our palates are saturated with a thirst for wanting, becoming, and doing more. More of what we need, more of what we do not, and less of what is healthy for the intricacies of our soulish man, *As It Pleases God*. So, what do we do? We pursue what seems or feels right, not realizing the entrapments are designed to trick us into not knowing *How To Please God* as we should. Only to go with the flow of whatever with whomever, leading us straight into the PIT with a blinded one-way ticket.

Yet, for a time such as this, based upon the Promises given to our Forefathers, God says, 'NOT SO!' Not now, and not ever! The UNVEILING is now; He is removing the blinders from those who desire to Spiritually See, Hear, and Speak, *As It Pleases Him*. For the record, the Kingdom of Heaven is our destination, having an OPEN TICKET for our Heaven on Earth Experience to complete our Divine Missions.

So, what do we need to do for this Spiritual Endeavor? No one is precisely the same! Thus, we must prepare ourselves *Spirit to Spirit* and *As It Pleases God*, according to our Predestined Blueprint with a *Divine Reach* inside and outside of ourselves.

The Divine Reach

The Divine Reach has placed us smack dab in the center of the Revelational Era of Divine Wisdom, Secrets, Knowledge, Understanding, and Power. Therefore, the way we think, our words, actions, reactions, and beliefs affect or infect us with or without our permission. Thus, we must become very careful regarding our charactorial behaviors, as well as the decisions we make on a moment-by-moment basis.

Going with the flow of ourselves or others without the Holy Trinity involved will inadvertently invoke *The Big Question*, 'How To Please God?' Not knowing amid querying ourselves, He has pleased us all along. For this reason, if we can reach beyond our self-imposed limitations hidden underneath the multifaceted layers of trauma, setbacks, biases, conditioning, or our something else, our BLESSINGS are already interwoven within them.

The Divine Reach is predicated on the way in which we process the questions we ask ourselves when no one is looking. Basically, this is the *What, When, Where, How, Why,* and

Who behind what we are doing, saying, or becoming. Doing things 'Just Because' will not cut it; we are called to a higher standard to be 'In The Know' about what is going on within us as well as outside of us. Although this may not be a big deal to most. Still, in the Eye of God, this is PRIMAL.

Why is this relevant in the Eye of God? They are linked to our reasonings...why we do what we do...why we do not do what we should...why we allow what we allow...why we do not allow what we should.

Unbeknown to most, our reasoning has everything to do with our seasoning, the lack thereof, and its overuse. Is this not why SALT is mentioned in the Bible as the Heavenly Choice of seasoning for mankind? Absolutely! Let us go deeper into *The Big Question* surrounding the *Salt of the Earth*.

Salt of the Earth

Blandness and dullness are not something that the human psyche likes. Why? Excitement is in our nature! Once it is suppressed or we become dull of hearing, it can release the beast from within due to trauma, pleasure, or pain. More importantly, if we do not know what to use to calm the beast from within, we are headed for a state of peril.

To be crystal clear, no one, and I mean no one, is exempt from this state of being. Nor are we exempt from our self-induced reasonings or justifications. Thus, we must become the *Salt of the Earth* to tame it, *As It Pleases God*.

Why do we need to tame the beast from within? Most of us who lack understanding deny the underlying beast, even when it is rising up in its full-grown state and is in plain sight. How can this happen? According to scripture, "*For the hearts of this people have grown dull. Their ears are hard of hearing, And their eyes they have closed, Lest they should see with their eyes and hear with their ears, Lest they should understand with their hearts and turn, So that I should heal them."* Matthew 13:15.

Do we really need healing from dullness? Absolutely! Have you ever tried cutting something with a dull knife...it makes slicing difficult and sometimes impossible, right? The same applies to dullness. Here is the scripture: *"If the ax is dull, and one does not sharpen the edge, Then he must use more strength; But wisdom brings success."* Ecclesiastes 10:10.

How do we make becoming the *Salt of the Earth* and our reasoning make sense? Our positive reasoning becomes the right amount of seasoning to our salt. In addition, it makes us palatable and gives us more of a reason to operate in grace, Divine Grace, to be exact. In contrast, our negative reasoning produces too much salt, ruining our savor with excuses and lies while using people, judging them, and leading them astray.

What does salt have to do with us in Earthen Vessels? In the Eye of God, we are the *Salt of the Earth*; therefore, it has everything to do with us, even if we do not understand it or how it relates to us in Earthen Vessels. In the same way that salt is from the earth, so are we! All in all, it means that we are CONJOINED for moderation. What does this mean? We need it, and it needs us according to Kingdom Standards and not man's.

Salt, from ancient times until now, has been highly valued for its preservative qualities and its ability to enhance flavor, preserve food, and prevent spoilage. And being that the human body contains a certain percentage of salt, it plays a crucial role in maintaining the body's proper physiological functions. For example, it is used in maintaining proper fluid balance, transmitting nerve impulses, regulating the water content in the body, helping to maintain proper blood pressure, and supporting muscle functions.

We are often taught that salt is bad, but without it, we malfunction. However, EXCESSIVE salt intake can lead to health problems such as high blood pressure, heart disease, and stroke. The goal is to understand the BALANCE of how it can work for us or against us. For this reason, we must get an understanding of it from a Divine Perspective.

What if we do not need a Divine Perspective on the *Salt of the Earth*? No one is exempt! Even if we feel that we are, know this: "*Everyone will be seasoned with fire, and every sacrifice will be seasoned with salt.*" Mark 9:49. The key is to know what to do when our numbers are called!

Here is the deal: In the Eye of God, salt is designed for us, and we are NOT designed for the salt. What does this mean? Salt is harvested for us, and we are not harvested for the salt, which means there is a Higher Calling of Spirituality in our lives. Please allow me to Spiritually Align: "*Salt is good, but if the salt has lost its flavor, how shall it be seasoned? It is neither fit for the land nor for the dunghill, but men throw it out. He who has ears to hear, let him hear!*" Luke 14:34-35. Therefore, we must learn how to become the *Salt of the Earth* for His Benefit and *As It Pleases Him* to ensure that the Spirit Man comes forth to regulate us Mentally, Physically, Emotionally, and Spiritually through our CONSCIENCE and INSTINCTS. Blasphemy, right? Wrong!

Salt will continue to be produced, doing what it is designed to do with or without us. Meanwhile, if we do not become the *Salt of the Earth* as intended or *As It Pleases God*, without its invaluable commodity, we will get roasted and toasted by not producing what is already. Nor will our consciences or instincts work as they should, making our Spiritual Compass unregulated to the point where we do not know what we should know. Then again, it may cause us to dabble in things that we should not.

Why would we dibble and dabble as Believers? The conscience or instincts are malnourished, causing the conviction process NOT to work properly. Is this Biblical? I would have it no other way. Jesus says, "*You are the salt of the earth; but if the salt loses its flavor, how shall it be seasoned? It is then good for nothing but to be thrown out and trampled underfoot by men."* Matthew 5:13. Simply put, once our conscience and instincts stop working as they should, we will have constant bouts of being used, abused, frustrated, traumatized, manipulated, ostracized, and so on.

Unfortunately, opting out of becoming the *Salt of the Earth* or upholding moral values, *As It Pleases God*, can hinder us, especially when calling evil good and good evil. On the contrary, when we use the *Salt of the Earth* as a metaphor without taking it to heart or understanding the importance of leading a life of integrity, kindness, gratefulness, humility, obedience, and righteousness, we will get mixed up, confused, and frustrated by default.

How can we get good and evil mixed up? It happens all the time without us becoming aware of it, or we hide the fact that we are dealing with this state of being. Here are a few reasons that we become mixed up, but not limited to such:

- ☐ Due to our discernment faculties becoming thwarted.
- ☐ When we use an overly salty tongue or words to proactively preserve our victims for the right time, victimize them at our leisure, or character assassinate them.
- ☐ When our fruits are mangled and rotten without knowing that they are.
- ☐ When we choose not to utilize the Fruits of the Spirit, especially when we have the option to do so.
- ☐ When we are constantly lying to ourselves and others.
- ☐ When we are consumed with putting on masks to cover up.
- ☐ When we are battling with jealousy, envy, pride, greed, coveting, or competitiveness without self-corrective measures in place.
- ☐ When we are consumed with selfishness instead of selflessness.

☐ When we do not add God into the equation of our lives.

We are called to bring flavor and goodness to the world around us. In addition, we are also commissioned to do our reasonable service to prevent moral decay and corruption on our behalf while doing our due diligence. For the record, becoming a positive and transformative presence is a doable feat, especially when doing things *As It Pleases God* with integrity, courage, and unwavering commitment. Even if you are not perfect, here are the Spiritual Seals on this matter:

☐ *"And every offering of your grain offering you shall season with salt; you shall not allow the salt of the covenant of your God to be lacking from your grain offering. With all your offerings you shall offer salt."* Ezekiel 43:24.

☐ *"Let your speech always be with grace, seasoned with salt, that you may know how you ought to answer each one."* Colossians 4:6.

Dealing with Judgment

We all have a sense of judgment, positively or negatively. Here is the secret: We must extend the judgment toward ourselves for EXAMINATION purposes with the use of the Fruits of the Spirit to create a positive or a win-win situation, *As It Pleases God*. When dealing with ourselves in such a manner, it is easier to proactively add Him into the equation instead of reactively or after the fact.

Now, for the judgment of others, it is only used to GOVERN in Wisdom, such as with King Solomon, the son of King David in the Bible. It is so easy to point the finger without having all the details, the truth, the facts, or God's take on the situation. I have found the best way to cast down judgment is to offer compassion, mercy, and forgiveness, even if one does not agree with the situation, behavior, or circumstance. Clearly, this does not allow one to become a pushover or come into agreement with them. Instead, it allows us to peel back the layers of our hidden prejudices that tend to cast down as opposed to building up.

How do we deal with constantly being judged? The factor of judgment is all around us, and we will never get away from it physically. It is indeed the physical aspects of an individual that give others a bird's-eye view of what is taking place from within. In my opinion, we become a victim of judgment when we do not understand that we have a FREE-WILL or when we misuse our FREE-WILL to victimize others.

According to the Heavenly of Heavens, judgment is designed to encourage, motivate, or empower us toward righteousness. It is not designed to discourage, disable, humiliate, or betray others out of selfishness, envy, jealousy, pride, or hatred. When we become truly accountable for our actions, reactions, words, thoughts, beliefs, and the lack thereof, we are better able to overcome our fears, we are better able to deal with rejection, we are better able to deal with the lack of recognition, we are better able to discipline ourselves, and we are better able to take responsibility for our lives without having to shift the blame to make ourselves appear as if we are more than what we are.

The reason why we should take advantage of The Divine Reach is that we are able to create, change, strategize, and maneuver on an Amateur or Elite Level, Mentally, Physically, Emotionally, and Spiritually. It does not matter what restrictions or disabilities we may have; it is still our responsibility to continue to seek knowledge and understanding, *As It Pleases God*. Then again, we can also settle for being a Spiritual Pauper to please ourselves.

Regardless of your choice, your strength lies in your ability to choose a circle of empowerment, not a circle of defeat! Always remember, an idle mind becomes the devil's playground. So, get busy doing something or get creative. There is always something to do. Now, if for some reason you do not know what to do, ask yourself fact-finding questions such as, but not limited to such:

- ☐ What can I do?
- ☐ When can I do it?
- ☐ Where can I do it?
- ☐ How can I do it?
- ☐ Why should I do it?
- ☐ Who will it help, inspire, mentor, or encourage?

In *Dealing with Judgment*, this will help us to become proactive in getting and staying busy. Now, on the other side of the coin, we must have a balance with God, ourselves, family, friends, etc. Regardless of whether we are seeking advice or motivation, we are required to give it as well. Here again, I suggest giving positive advice or feedback to build, as opposed to tearing down.

Dealing with Assumptions

As we look over our lives, we often become defeated by the questions we avoid asking or the ones we do not know how to ask. Throughout my Spiritual Journey, I have had to learn how to ask a lot of questions to get an understanding, which often offends those who do not like to be questioned. With my mindset, I am like: 'How do I know if I do not ask?' They are like: 'Why is she questioning me?' The bottom line is that assumptions have placed us in the position that we are in today.

Dealing with Assumptions is an inherent part of our human nature, shaping our perceptions, thoughts, beliefs, desires, words, decisions, and interactions on a daily basis; however, they are not always dependable, applicable, or relevant. Although assumptions fill in the GAPS in our understanding, *The Big Question* is, 'Why would we leave such a gap when it takes the same amount of energy to ask fact-finding questions?'

What is the big deal about asking questions, especially when we are taught to mind our business? The deal is that Hosea 4:6 says, *"My people are destroyed for lack of knowledge."* Plus, minding our business and asking relevant fact-finding questions to avoid assumptions are two different things.

In the Eye of God, when assuming without inquiry, we place ourselves in a peculiar position with Him. Why? God will not trust us with the Treasures, Wisdom, and Secrets of the Kingdom when we are prone to making assumptions or jumping to conclusions without asking relevant fact-finding questions.

Are we not all prone to assuming? Absolutely! As long as we have breath in our bodies, we are all subjected to human behaviors, reasonings, and tendencies. Still, we do not have to allow our assumptions to become a forbidden, deceptive, or assumptive fruit, a reason to cover our nakedness, nor should we bring our names to shame.

Here is the deal: Having an assumption or clearing an assumption and acting upon it are not the same in the Eye of God. Frankly, this is why 1 John 4:1 advises: *"Beloved, do not believe every spirit, but test the spirits, whether they are of God; because many false prophets have gone out into the world."*

What if we do not opt to test the Spirit behind the assumption? We can 'get got' by reason of omission. Plus, we run the risk of perpetuating stereotypes and prejudices by assuming.

Why do we become an at-risk Believer? First, assumptions can shape our perceptions positively or negatively. Secondly, unexamined assumptions can lead to misunderstandings, conflicts, judging, and missed opportunities. Thirdly, by acknowledging our assumptions and actively seeking to validate or challenge them by asking relevant fact-finding questions, we can gain a deeper understanding of ourselves and others without forcing our mindsets, thought sets, biases, or opinions on them. Here is a checklist to remind us why we should not assume and ask questions, but not limited to such:

☐ Assumptions can lead to misunderstanding, misinterpretation, miscommunication, monopolies, and malpractice.

☐ Making assumptions can limit the ability to respectfully understand others and their perspectives. Then again, it may cause us to stub or violate someone's free will or individuality.

☐ Assumptions can lead to missed opportunities for learning, understanding, and growth from those appearing above or beneath us.

☐ Assumptions can hinder effective collaboration, articulation, and teamwork, causing us to become lone rangers.

☐ Making assumptions about others can create barriers and wedges in building meaningful relationships, resulting in self-sabotage, soul ties, and unfair ultimatums.

☐ Assumptions can result in unfair treatment or trauma based on unfounded beliefs, unforgiveness, vendettas, unresolved issues, or biases.

- [ ] Assumptions can contribute to a lack of empathy, mercy, forgiveness, compassion, and understanding while character-assassinating ourselves and others.

- [ ] Assumptions can lead to decision-making based on incomplete, false, or inaccurate information, contributing to many regrets and constantly playing cleanup.

- [ ] Assumptions may result in judgmental attitudes and behaviors toward others, making us contentious and hard to deal with.

- [ ] Assumptions can perpetuate a closed-minded approach to new ideas and experiences, contributing to our missing the mark, missing out on great information, or not recognizing the BLESSING.

- [ ] Making assumptions can undermine the principle of treating others with respect, kindness, and dignity, contributing to a trail of rotten fruit following behind us.

- [ ] Assumptions can hinder personal and professional growth, knowledge, understanding, and wisdom as we remain in a state of confusion or stuntedness.

- [ ] Making assumptions can contribute to distrust and division, causing us to falsely accuse those who are innocent without seeking the TRUTH.

- [ ] Assumptions can perpetuate confusion, violence, chaos, and confusion. Meanwhile, becoming a belligerent fire-starter or instigator through lies, projection, and deflection without engaging in self-reflection, *As It Pleases God.*

- ☐ Assumptions can weaken our ability to develop a *Spirit to Spirit* Relationship with God, our Heavenly Father.

Now that we have *Dealing with Assumptions* out of the way, *The Ultimate Question* is, 'How do we please God?' Better yet, does anyone have the answer to this question outside of God Almighty? Some would say 'yes,' and others would say 'no.'

Whether we realize it or not, we have the answer hidden within us when dealing with *The Big Question.* Yet, amid answering, for starters, we also must know WHY we are serving Him and WHAT displeases Him. Without genuinely understanding Kingdom Principles and Protocols *As It Pleases God*, we become subject to our own understanding on our terms instead of His. Unfortunately, this contributes to us becoming easily swayed, brainwashed, or uncovered, misgoverning our likes and dislikes with the lust of the eyes, the lust of the flesh, and the pride of life while appearing right or justified.

Remove the Plank

According to the Heavenly of Heavens, in this Movement of God, *As It Pleases Him*, all is not lost. However, it behooves us to consider how we please ourselves or what is causing Spiritual Disappointment in the Eye of God. Nevertheless, amid all, it is imperative to *Remove the Plank* from our own eyes. Matthew 7:5 says that we must: *"First remove the plank from your own eye, and then you will see clearly to remove the speck from your brother's eye."*

Doing your checkups from the neck up or conducting a self-analysis from the inside out is good for you, especially when trying to avoid becoming a plankster (slinging dirt into the eyes of others) or a prankster (playing games). Here are a few ways to pinpoint hidden planks or specks in your eye, but not limited to such:

- ☐ Reflect on your own shortcomings.
- ☐ Take note of your biases and words.
- ☐ Practice self-awareness.
- ☐ Seek feedback from others about your behavior.
- ☐ Engage in regular self-reflection.
- ☐ Evaluate yourself and your thoughts continually.
- ☐ Consider seeking counseling or therapy.
- ☐ Address your personal issues.
- ☐ Read books and articles on self-improvement.
- ☐ Document your personal growth.
- ☐ Cultivate a growth mindset.
- ☐ Become open to learning from your mistakes.
- ☐ Take responsibility for your actions.
- ☐ Identify negative patterns in your behavior.
- ☐ Set personal development goals.
- ☐ Assess and align your values and beliefs for consistency.
- ☐ Seek out mentors or role models.
- ☐ Acknowledge your limitations
- ☐ Become open to seeking help when needed.
- ☐ Avoid making assumptions.
- ☐ Gather all relevant information.
- ☐ Make good and sound decisions.
- ☐ Engage in acts of kindness and compassion.
- ☐ Use the Fruits of the Spirit.

Using this list while simultaneously asking the right questions to MASTER *How To Please God* will change the trajectory of your life. How so? When positioning yourself for success, this list can position you to become teachable and trainable when used properly and according to your Divinely Blueprinted Purpose.

By positioning oneself to become teachable and trainable, *As It Pleases God* opens the psyche to new ideas, perspectives, knowledge, understandings, and queries. Conversely, by not asking the right questions or deceiving ourselves creates a disservice from the inside out.

Why would we create a disservice when we are doing our best? The interpretation of Spirituality has become diluted, polluted, and convoluted because we have not come to the Divine Unveiling of Kingdom Absolutes. Plus, asking the same cookie-cutter questions means something is wrong with our genetic makeup. Nonetheless, if we dare to set aside our preconceived notions and ego-driven resistance in order to absorb valuable Divine Insights, *As It Pleases God*, it will revolutionize our lives.

For example, when vetting a relationship, if we take a list of questions to query a potential partner without knowing who we are from the inside out or proceeding without the Holy Spirit, it could become a recipe for disaster. Why? First, if we do not know who we are, we will attract someone to define us instead of complimenting us, *As It Pleases God*. Unfortunately, this often leads us away from the Purpose of God, which invokes insecurities, disobedience, planks, and a victim mentality over time. Secondly, the enemy is the master of deception and disguises, telling us everything we want to hear until we are venomously yoked.

What is wrong with asking fact-finding questions? To be clear, we should ask questions; there is nothing wrong with querying. However, we should ask ourselves more questions and get to know ourselves better than anyone else. Why should we know ourselves better than anyone else? We all have strengths and weaknesses, and do not want to fall victim to the cookie-cutter one-way mentality or resort to playing mind games. What is the big deal, especially when we have free will to ask, say, and do whatever with whomever? It fogs up our Spiritual Mirror, preventing us from clearly seeing or understanding ourselves or our motives.

In the Eye of God, mind games cause us to play ourselves short, fall short in our PEOPLE SKILLS, selfishly please ourselves, develop wrong motives, or become consumed with judgment. And sometimes, all of this is done in the Name of God as we weaponize or prostitute Him for gain or our benefit. Is this really happening? Absolutely! More than we care to imagine, as we seek to control everything or everyone within our circle of grasp.

Here again, when someone attempts to vet me using lists or mind games to determine my worthiness, I find a way to avoid, redirect, or counteract trap questions. Doing so allows them to pass judgment, play mind games, or manipulate me like I am boo boo the fool, insulting my intelligence. Why would I not simply answer the questions or allow this to happen, wasting precious time? First, it makes a great story, lesson, or Divine Wisdom for the Kingdom. Secondly, I am a master communicator, making RELEVANCY crucial. Why? Because I see, hear, extract, convert, and articulate what most cannot. Therefore, I need the stories, experiences, lessons, and understanding to pinpoint what we need to discuss. And thirdly, casting my pearls among the swine will cause me to 'get got,' detouring me from doing what I am called to do, *As It Pleases God*.

I do not speak just to hear myself talk or convince others about who I am and why. My character, fruits, and humility speak louder than the questions asked or the tests used to break or prank me. More importantly, if the Holy Spirit did not forewarn them about me or my method of operation, nor would I. Plus, if they decide I am NOT worthy enough to be in their circle, I keep it moving in the Spirit of Excellence, shaking the dust off my feet with a smile.

Then, once the dust settles, guess who wants a do-over or is longing for a conversation with me? For this reason, we must be cautious about who we judge, insult, walk over, step on, reject, or kick when they are down. Remember, in the Kingdom of God, our BLESSINGS will never appear as such; they are often presented in seed form or as a diamond in the rough.

When dealing with *The Big Question*, talk is cheap. But according to the Heavenly of Heavens, our character is PROFOUND. For this reason, we must become a MASTER at questioning ourselves first, allowing people to be who they are. In the Eye of God, this lets us know what we are dealing with. Is this Biblical? I would have it no other way. *"Beware of false prophets, who come to you in sheep's clothing, but inwardly they are ravenous wolves. You will know them by their fruits. Do men gather grapes from thornbushes or figs from thistles? Therefore by their fruits you will know them."* Matthew 7:15-16, 20. Once we develop this mindset, we can better use Spiritual Principles, *As It Pleases God*, to remove our hidden, open, or unknown planks.

Why must we remove our self-induced planks when dealing with *The Big Question*? Simply put, *"Can the blind lead the blind? Will they not both fall into the ditch?"* Luke 6:39. When dealing with Spiritual Principles, no one is exempt from blindness; we must work on ourselves consistently with a work-in-progress mentality. What makes this so important in the Eye of God? *"A disciple is not above his teacher, but everyone who is perfectly trained will be like his teacher."* Luke 6:40.

We cannot pretend to understand if we do not understand something or someone. Actually, pretending to understand creates confusion, and it breaks the bond of trust. For example, as The WHY Doctor, I am very forgiving, and I understand who God has created me to be. Being that we do not all think alike, if I lack understanding or the ability to relate to something or someone, I will admit it politely to seek clarity.

In addition, I will also find a way to ask the right questions to avoid assuming or to avoid misunderstanding. In my opinion, a misunderstood assumption is a quick way to get our truth or their truth WRONG! Here are a few ways I would convey my inability to understand:

- ☐ I do not understand what is taking place right now, but I trust God for Divine Wisdom and Understanding. [Then ask fact-finding questions in the *What, When, Where, How, Why,* or with *Whom* formation.]

- ☐ I cannot relate to or understand this sort of behavior, nor will I tolerate it. Please allow me to excuse myself. [Then ask fact-finding questions in the *What, When, Where, How, Why,* or with *Whom* formation.]

- ☐ I do not understand what is being said. Please allow me to gain clarification. [Then ask fact-finding questions in the *What, When, Where, How, Why,* or with *Whom* formation.]

- ☐ I am trying to understand this situation; therefore, I need to ask a few more questions. [Then ask fact-finding questions in the *What, When, Where, How, Why,* or with *Whom* formation.]

- ☐ Just so we are clear. I need further explanation about what is being said. [Then ask fact-finding questions in the *What, When, Where, How, Why,* or with *Whom* formation.]

- [ ] I am struggling to grasp the concept. Could you please elaborate on what you said? [Then ask fact-finding questions in the *What, When, Where, How, Why*, or with *Whom* formation.]

- [ ] For some reason, this is not clicking for me; therefore, I am seeking more clarity on what was said. [Then ask fact-finding questions in the *What, When, Where, How, Why*, or with *Whom* formation.]

- [ ] I am having a hard time wrapping my head around this concept. [Then ask fact-finding questions in the *What, When, Where, How, Why*, or with *Whom* formation.]

- [ ] I am finding it difficult to follow along. Can you provide more details on what you mentioned? [Then ask fact-finding questions in the *What, When, Where, How, Why*, or with *Whom* formation.]

- [ ] I cannot seem to make sense of this. Please allow me to gain clarity. [Then ask fact-finding questions in the *What, When, Where, How, Why*, or with *Whom* formation.]

- [ ] I am not quite grasping this. Can you expound on what you mentioned? [Then ask fact-finding questions in the *What, When, Where, How, Why*, or with *Whom* formation.]

- [ ] I am feeling lost in trying to understand. Could you shed more light on what you said? [Then ask fact-finding questions in the *What, When, Where, How, Why*, or with *Whom* formation.]

- [ ] I am having trouble making sense of it. Can you offer more details about what you said? [Then ask fact-finding questions in the *What, When, Where, How, Why,* or with *Whom* formation.]

☐ I am not quite getting the hang of it. Can you explain what you said in more detail? [Then ask fact-finding questions in the *What, When, Where, How, Why,* or with *Whom* formation.]

☐ Unfortunately, this is just not registering with me. Could you give me a more detailed explanation of what you said? [Then ask fact-finding questions in the *What, When, Where, How, Why,* or with *Whom* formation.]

☐ I feel like I am missing a few pieces to the puzzle. Please allow me to gain clarity in this matter. [Then ask fact-finding questions in the *What, When, Where, How, Why,* or with *Whom* formation.]

☐ I am not quite seeing the whole picture yet. Can you break it down for me? [Then ask fact-finding questions in the *What, When, Where, How, Why,* or with *Whom* formation.]

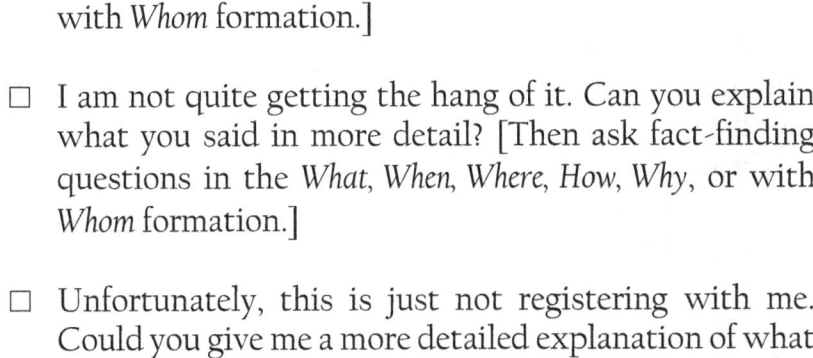

Violating our conscience or pretending to be someone other than who we are is EXHAUSTING. It is also stressful, especially when we have to continue to play a role out of our original positive or negative character. For me, when I have to exhibit tough love, it hurts.

Why would it hurt to exhibit tough love? It hurts because I want to give in, I want to be kind, I want to be helpful, I want to be loving, I want to be nurturing, I want to be inspiring, etc. Still, in order to protect myself, my Gift, my Anointing, my Legacy, and my *Signature Effect*, or to keep their Spiritual Plank from becoming mine, there are times when I have to say 'NO' and mean it!

What is so tough about saying 'no' to someone? For me, toughness is not being abrasive or rough around the edges. Nor does it make me weak or a pushover; it is about exhibiting the Fruits of the Spirit and protecting them at all costs. What is really tough is when I have to say 'yes' when I want to say 'no' to someone or something to protect the integrity of my Spiritual Fruits.

Why do I need to protect the Fruits of the Spirit? Or, better yet, can the Fruits of the Spirit not take care of themselves? Absolutely. The Fruits of the Spirit can indeed hold their own; however, it is my responsibility to do the Spiritual Inspection while exhibiting SELF-CONTROL to keep my *Signature Effect* intact in the Spirit of Righteousness.

Then again, regardless of the hard decisions that must be made, I am on a Spiritual Assignment, *As It Pleases God*, doing what I am called to do, according to my Predestined Blueprint. Now, *The Big Question* is, 'What about you?'

CHAPTER 2
SIGNATURE EFFECT

A re you Heavenly Endorsed? Do you have a desire to become endorsed by the Heavenly of Heavens? Do you think it is even possible for Heaven and Earth to endorse you? Well, let me say this: 'It is possible and probable, especially when you are in HARMONY with them both simultaneously!'

What would it take to get that *Signature Effect*? First, it takes INTERCONNECTEDNESS with a *Spirit to Spirit* Relationship with our Heavenly Father. Secondly, we must approach Him with respect and without defying the natural order or rhythm of things. In return, with the Spiritual Endorsement and *As It Pleases God*, it will grant us Divine Strength, Favor, Protection, and Guidance, containing a *Signature Effect* uncommon to most and possessed only by a few. But do not worry, if one is reading this book, you are one of the few...just follow the instructions, *As It Pleases God*, without trying to please yourself or showboat.

Then again, how would we become the Crème de la Crème amid our imperfections? The simple answer would be through Spiritually Aligning our character to *As It Pleases God* instead of pleasing ourselves and using the Fruits of the Spirit.

According to the Ancient of Days, for the *Signature Effect*, having God sign off on our Breastplate of Righteousness, first and foremost, we cannot place Him in a box or limit Him. Secondly, we must seek to understand and fulfill our unique PURPOSE and POTENTIAL using our Spiritual Gifts. Thirdly, from His Divine Perspective, the BEST WAY to have Him sign off or provide us with a Spiritual Seal is to develop a personal *Spirit to Spirit* Relational Connection, use the Fruits of the Spirit, and behave Christlike.

With or without *Signature Effects* or Spiritual Seals, we all have different wants, needs, desires, conditionings, traumas, and our psyches standing in the way. As a result of our humanity, we CANNOT pinpoint a definitive list of ways to please God; we CANNOT think we are above Him, and we dare not think we have Him pegged.

Why can we not have a finite list of pinpointing or pegging God? First, God is not a science project, nor are His ways ours. According to the Tower of Babel, when exhibiting this behavior, He will change the Spiritual Language on site and at the drop of a dime. Genesis 11:1-9 is where God intervened by confounding their language. As a result, the confusion led to the abandonment of the tower's construction and the dispersal of the people into different nations and tribes. This event is known as the 'confusion of tongues,' and in today's time, it is also an indication of disobedience or pompousness.

To make the Tower of Babel relevant and timely, here are a few reasons why God will change our Spiritual Language, but not limited to these reasons:

- ☐ To prevent us from exuding defiance of His Divine Will.
- ☐ To scatter us to refocus our attention.
- ☐ To prevent us from uniting or plotting against Him.
- ☐ To create cultural diversity among different nations.
- ☐ To prevent a centralized power from dominating.
- ☐ To humble humanity.
- ☐ To prevent excessive pride and arrogance.

- ☐ To test and strengthen the faith.
- ☐ To develop the resilience of humanity.
- ☐ To prevent the misuse of a Spiritual Language.
- ☐ To break us from using Him for nefarious purposes.
- ☐ To emphasize the importance of communication.
- ☐ To develop an understanding of something or someone.
- ☐ To promote development.
- ☐ To establish the consequences of human arrogance.
- ☐ To prevent the concentration of knowledge and power.
- ☐ To promote exploration and discovery.
- ☐ To emphasize the value of cooperation.
- ☐ To develop a mutual understanding of diverse groups.
- ☐ To lay the foundation of a knowledgeable system.
- ☐ To demonstrate God's authority and sovereignty.
- ☐ To prevent the misuse of innocent people.
- ☐ To teach humility, empathy, and cooperation.
- ☐ To break the Spirit of Nimrod (outsmarting God) off us.

The Spirit of Defiance is real. If this negative ambition is left unchecked, it will create a downfall or some form of scattering for us when we least expect it. For the record, a united vision can become our downfall when we think we are above God Almighty, as if our putrified efforts do not stink.

Listen, we will never see from God's Perspective if we do not have Spiritual Eyes to see, *As It Pleases Him*. If we do not have Spiritual Ears, we will never hear Divine Instructions, Wisdom, or Revelation, *As It Pleases Him*. More importantly, if we do not acclimate ourselves to the Resonating Sound of God, our Spiritual Voice will not penetrate the Heavenly of Heavens as it should.

For the above reasons, God requires discipline, obedience, humility, and patience to *Please Him* wholeheartedly. With those, He can work out the kinks in His Spiritual Classroom with the Vicissitudes, Cycles, Seasons, and Seeds of Life. On the other hand, if we decide to remain undisciplined, uncorrected, rebellious, prideful, impatient, or rude, we are left to our own reasonings, excuses, and justifications as they please us. Unfortunately, these are all funneled through our dubious acts, thoughts, and beliefs of selfishness, while appearing right in our own eyes.

How can we break the bonds of selfishness? Become selfless, humble, repenting, forgiving, and *GRATEFUL*.

Gratefulness

When it comes to *Gratefulness*, we should avoid pinpointing or pegging God because we all have a unique Divine Blueprint or Mission, and He is the Creator of it all. Without Him, there is NOTHING...so GRATEFULNESS should be our portion.

Why should we be grateful, especially when we have it going on? When we think we are above Him, rest assured in due time, He will bring shame to our names or remove Spiritual Seals if we have them, similar to the King Saul Experience. Spiritually Speaking, we must exercise extreme caution in this area.

Why should we exhibit caution when thinking we are above God Almighty? In the Eye of God, only hidden or open insecurities would cause us to think we are above Him. Remember, He prewired our DNA, and if the mind does not naturally RESPECT or give REVERENCE, there is a Spiritual Glitch in the Divine System. So do not be fooled!

Even the Devil knows how to REVERENCE God Almighty. How can an oppositional force answer to God? Did He not seek permission from God to afflict Job? He knows and uses the Bible and Spiritual Principles better than Believers, banking on our not knowing what to do or how to do it. Unfortunately, getting us to do His bidding, the dirty work, turning on ourselves, or pointing the finger. All of which unravels our Spiritual Seals.

Instead, we should take responsibility, learning, growing, and sowing back into the Kingdom, *As It Pleases God*, reinforcing our Divine Seals to invoke the *Signature Effect*. If one does not know this, one will 'get got' by omitting *Gratefulness*, not covering oneself with the Blood of Jesus, and failing to utilize the Holy Spirit as one should.

What is the big deal about gratitude, especially when content or satisfied with our lives? Without *Gratefulness*, it leads to the breeding ground of hatefulness, which is often undetected until it is fully grown and securely rooted within the human psyche. All we need to do is check our thoughts, inner chatter, and spoken words. They tell a story, and if we do not interject *Gratefulness* or create a win-win, our story will become a yoke-in-progress instead of a work-in-progress, *As It Pleases God*.

In theory, when knowing nothing about God or His Spiritual Principles, saying THANK YOU only takes a fraction of a second. Yet, according to the Heavenly of Heavens, authentic *Gratefulness* is one of the most overlooked commodities known to man. How could this be? It just is...take a look around; it is in plain sight; we have become robotic with gestures of gratitude.

How have we become robotic? Roboticism is detected in our actions, biases, thoughts, and beliefs that DO NOT ALIGN with what comes from our mouths. Often, this is when we say one thing and do another. Or, when we say something that we are conditioned to say, such as 'I love you,' 'I believe in you,' or 'Thank you,' but do not mean it or are just being polite.

Nevertheless, to counteract the roboticism we presently face, we should include elements of gratitude in our gestures. For example, 'Thank you for doing a great job today.' 'Thank you for helping me understand the paperwork.' 'Thank you for your kindness.' 'God, thank you for allowing me to wake up, breathing the Breath of Life.' 'God, I appreciate this experience; what do I need to learn or glean from this?' 'Thank you for the experience; I learned a valuable lesson I must share with others on my Spiritual Journey.' More importantly, and unbeknown to most, gestures of gratitude have enough POWER to change our lives if we use and align them, *As They Please God!*

In addition, we should avoid pinpointing or pegging God due to varying religions and belief systems with different perspectives, contending to be the Chosen Elect. For this reason, God weighs the hearts and motives of all mankind, even with superficial facades in place. However, living a virtuous life, treating others with kindness and respect, practicing gratitude, extending forgiveness, repenting often, and engaging in acts of service or charity with clean hands and a pure heart earns us *Divine Favor*. Here is a checklist of a few ways to up the ante on *Gratefulness*, but not limited to such:

- ☐ Begin and end each day with a prayer of thanks.
- ☐ Pray for Divine Guidance and Illumination.
- ☐ Repent, forgive, and seek wisdom daily.
- ☐ Pray for those who are less fortunate.
- ☐ Develop a *Spirit to Spirit* Relationship with God.
- ☐ Cover yourself with the Blood of Jesus.
- ☐ Usher in the Holy Spirit.
- ☐ Use the Fruits of the Spirit.
- ☐ Help those in need and share with others.
- ☐ Attend church services.
- ☐ Spend time in nature.
- ☐ Embrace challenges as opportunities for growth.
- ☐ Show kindness and love.
- ☐ Read and meditate on scriptures.
- ☐ Reflect on God's goodness.
- ☐ Sing praises and worship songs.

- ☐ Use your talents and skills to serve others.
- ☐ Say 'thank you' often and mean it.
- ☐ Let go of grudges.
- ☐ Trust in God's plan and provision.

Divine Favor

Do you think that favor is fair? Do you know the difference between normal favor and *Divine Favor*? Then again, do you think they are the same? Well, as you know...if I am posing this question, then they may not be the same. One is man-endorsed with conditions, and the other is Heavenly Endorsed with contingencies.

How do we receive *Divine Favor* amid imperfections? When dealing with Spiritual Absolutes, *As It Pleases God*, it is based upon the Spiritual Law of Seedtime and Harvest, which is the Law of Reciprocity, and our PEOPLE SKILLS with outright humility, good motives, teachability, and positive fruits. If we are Spiritually Usable in the Eye of God, we will receive more favor than those who are rebellious, disobedient, or stiff-necked. Even if we are a work-in-progress, we must remain on the positive side of the spectrum in all things while consistently self-correcting, repenting, and making our best attempts to become better, stronger, and wiser.

Suppose we do not remain positive or do not know how. When remaining stuck on the negative without self-correcting, repenting, or justifying and making excuses not to do what needs to be done, *As It Pleases God*, we will find ourselves on a constant cycle of déjà vu. Unfortunately, we will remain in this state with varying characters until we learn the lessons needed to elevate to the next level or align with our Predestined Blueprint. Simply put, we have the same issues with different people, making it evident that the issue is not with them but within us. In reality, they are on assignment without knowing it, as we are stuck in a Spiritual

Classroom, refusing to learn and taking remedial courses while thinking we have it going on.

To avoid a remedial status in the Eye of God, we must know the difference between positive and negative character traits. Why do we need to know the difference, especially when thoroughly educated? Most pretend they know but do not! As a result, they create a disservice to themselves and others, causing them to miss out on the Fruits of the Spirit and Christlike Character, *As It Pleases God*, only to please themselves.

For example, in the Eye of God, I am held at a higher accountability than most because I am Spiritually Trained, Commissioned, and Anointed in Spiritual Principles and Divine Wisdom. For this reason, with Divine Revelation, Detection, Protection, and Correction on my side, I cannot get down with anything or be dragged into a mess to lose my Kingdom Status or *Signature Effect* for frivolous folly. So, when I disagree with someone or interject positivity to counteract a negative, for someone NOT knowing the difference between the two, they would inadvertently think I am being negative or condescending. Then again, they may interpret it as trying to fix them or being overly Spiritual based on their perception of my disagreement.

Here is the deal: I kindly disagreed by interjecting a fact, truth, understanding, reversing the negative into a positive on the spot, or asking a fact-finding question, getting them to THINK or LISTEN to what they were conveying. In this disagreement scenario, I did not say a negative word, behave negatively, project a negative thought, or become confrontational. While approaching, *As It Pleases God*, and in their best interest, my intents were misappropriated, misunderstood, or misaligned by them, not knowing the difference between positive and negative characteristics. As a result, it caused them to miss the Spiritual Elements of Divine Wisdom altogether.

Understandably, we are all entitled to our perceptional opinion, but motives carry the Spiritual Weight in our Kingdom or worldly efforts. To say the least, God sent them the information they needed to self-correct. But they could not hear it properly because they misinterpreted it as negative when it was DIVINE. Unfortunately, this is how we 'get got' to the highest degree!

At times, my non-participation in debaucherous efforts results in facing ridicule, rejection, and isolation. Nevertheless, I am unwavering in my commitment to maintaining my Spiritual Integrity, refusing to lose my *Divine Favor* or fall short of penetrating the hearts of those who desire to learn *How To Please God* for real.

With *Divine Favor*, we are in this together, redirecting all things back to our Heavenly Father with *Kingdom Absolutes* as we "*Let all things be done decently and in order.*" 1 Corinthians 14:40.

Kingdom Absolutes

Kingdom Absolutes from God's Divine Perspective refer to Divine Principles, Laws, or Truths that are considered unchanging, unwavering, certain, non-negotiable, and universal. In Divine Understanding and Authority, these absolutes are fundamental to God's nature and are not influenced by external factors. For example, Divine Love, Justice, and Truth are perceived as unwavering within God's Divine Nature. Whereas with our nature, we place conditions on love, justice, and truth based on our perceptions, biases, reasonings, traumas, favoritism, and so on.

According to the Ancient of Days, with *Kingdom Absolutes*, we are all created differently with unique fingerprints. If we are robotically questioning ourselves without involving God, it symbolizes not aligning with our Predestined Blueprint, even if we pretend we are. For this reason, once achieving a goal, we instantly become ungrateful, unsatisfied, unfulfilled, or insecure by default, regardless of our achievements, status, fame, or fortune. What causes this to happen? We must involve God in our life's equation, *As It Pleases Him*, with an openness to our Divine Blueprinted Purpose, and use *Kingdom Absolutes* known as Spiritual Laws, Principles, and Concepts.

What do *Kingdom Absolutes* mean to Believers? Outside of the Kingdom Mentality, *As It Pleases God*, we change based upon our opinions, biases, feelings, thoughts, conditioning, traumas, influences, or beliefs. Whereas, with God Almighty, He is just, He does not change, He is not wishy-washy, and He is NOT inconsistent as we are outside of Him. Yet, amid all His Spiritual Laws and Absolutes, He is still MERCIFUL, providing a way of escape!

What is the way of escape? The way of escape is a two-edged sword, with our fruits, character, motives, trust, and beliefs providing a way to or away from God or the Kingdom. And being subject to change on a whim, we must be cognizant of how we behave, treat, and respect others in public and behind closed doors. Blasphemy, right? Wrong. *"Therefore let him who thinks he stands take heed lest he fall. No temptation has overtaken you except such as is common to man; but God is faithful, who will not allow you to be tempted beyond what you are able, but with the temptation will also make the way of escape, that you may be able to bear it. Therefore, my beloved, flee from idolatry. I speak as to wise men; judge for yourselves what I say. The cup of blessing which we bless, is it not the communion of the blood of Christ? The bread which we break, is it not the communion of the body of Christ? For we, though many, are one bread and one body; for we all partake of that one bread."* 1 Corinthians 10:12-17.

Why must we examine our behaviors, thoughts, beliefs, and character, *As It Pleases God*? When representing the Kingdom of Heaven or desiring the *Signature Effect*, negativity Mentally, Physically, and Emotionally can taint us with jealousy, envy, pride, greed, coveting, competitiveness, and revenge, causing us to waver in our faith or become manipulative. Please allow me to align, "*Let your conduct be without covetousness; be content with such things as you have. For He Himself has said, 'I will never leave you nor forsake you.' So we may boldly say: 'The LORD is my helper; I will not fear. What can man do to me?' Remember those who rule over you, who have spoken the word of God to you, whose faith follow, considering the outcome of their conduct. Jesus Christ is the same yesterday, today, and forever."* Hebrews 13:5-8.

The Portion

Pleasing God may not be our cup of tea, but in the Eye of God, it is unmistakably our PORTION to Spiritually Seal our reason for being. What is our PORTION? It is the Spiritual Rationing, Inheritance, or Reflection of using:

- ☐ **P**atience.
- ☐ **O**bedience.
- ☐ **R**epentance.
- ☐ **T**eachability.
- ☐ **I**ntegrity.
- ☐ **O**vercoming.
- ☐ **N**urturing.

As a Wave Offering, utilizing the Holy Trinity, *As It Pleases Him*, build our FAITH in God, ourselves, and others, allowing us to be who we are and others to be who they are without manipulating people, places, and things to cater to our agenda.

Why is PORTIONING so important when learning *How To Please God*? Most of us do not know our reason for being, only going with the flow to fit in or avoid becoming outcasts. At the same time, having NO Gift, Calling, Talent, Creativity, or

Purpose to use as a Wave Offering or Spiritual Tool for Him to feed His sheep. Nor do we present them as a Sweet Aroma memorializing Gratefulness or workability. Here is what we must know: *"Then the priest shall take from the grain offering a memorial portion, and burn it on the altar. It is an offering made by fire, a sweet aroma to the LORD."* Leviticus 2:9. Although this is in the Old Testament, it has not lost its power or potency; we simply must learn how to use it according to today's standards from God's Divine Perspective. Why? *"For the LORD's portion is His people; Jacob is the place of His inheritance."* Deuteronomy 32:9.

Knowing what we are designed to do, *As It Pleases God*, leads to fewer disappointments, fewer shattered dreams, fewer occurrences of lost hope, and less time spent playing the blaming game. On the other hand, it can also usher us into self-discovery, fulfillment, Double Portions, and Divine Opportunities, aligning with our Predestined Blueprints, even amid our idiosyncrasies, hidden traumas, or underlying uniqueness. What does this mean for us in the Eye of God? We do not need to be perfect, just USABLE.

The goal of this book is to usher you into a *Spirit to Spirit* Relationship with your Heavenly Father. Why? It is designed to help you download SPECIFIC INSTRUCTIONS or DETAILS according to your Divine Blueprint with an UNDERSTANDING. However, before doing so or manifesting, you must acquire the vital strategies outside your ordinary prayer and worship sessions, making it personal and intentional, *As It Pleases God*. With this approach to personal development, you can gain Divine Access from the Heavenly of Heavens that most can only dream about having, enabling Divine Intervention and Alignment to work on your behalf and in your favor. If this book has made it into your hands or your presence, reach your hand out to me as we do this TOGETHER as ONE TEAM with a PROMISE that you will never be or think the same again.

CHAPTER 3
RESONATING SOUND

We often do not use the word resonate much, but the *Resonating Sound* never ceases in the Kingdom of Heaven. Realistically speaking, this is similar to how the Earth rotates on its Axis; if it jumped off, we are in deep trouble, right? Absolutely. The same applies to the *Resonating Sounds* hidden within each of us. Once we stop vibrating or moving, *As It Pleases God*, we become internally lost by default based upon our DNA, Bloodline, or Divine Purpose. With the hidden desire to reconnect, our psyche will inadvertently buffer with hiccups, letting us know that there is more to us and preventing us from totally forgetting.

For example, babies are still connected to the *Resonating Sounds* when they are born, gradually disconnecting over a period of time. For this reason, we will see them laugh, smirk, look, or watch those Spiritually Sound and reject or avoid those disdainly wicked. So, we should not downplay the days of small beginnings because babies can do what grownups cannot.

Why do babies notice what their parents cannot? They are still connected with their instincts at full alert, going on vibrational sounds, especially after spending nine months in their mother's tummy, going on instincts alone with the inability to speak audibly.

As It Pleases God, Divine Wisdom does not LOOK like what we think; it RESONATES within the human psyche. What does this mean? It is not a LOOK; it is a VIBRATION in the sound. Just as animals hear, understand, and communicate through vibrational measures, we can too, but we must be Spiritually Trained to do so, even though we were born with this ability.

What is the purpose of losing our *Resonating Sound*? We do not lose it; it becomes dormant or hidden under our layers of something else. If we do not understand the longing to connect back to the Source and our Predestined Blueprint (our reason for being), we will begin to fill up on worldly people, places, and things. Then again, we will gravitate toward anything catering to the lust of the eyes, the lust of the flesh, and the pride of life to feed the senses of the psyche or spin our superficial axis, dulling our authentic Spiritual Voice.

What is the big deal, especially when we are here to enjoy life? Enjoying life is a matter of perception. Listen, if our enjoyment is destroying us, how enjoyable is that? We can have the best of both in our Heaven on Earth Experience; we simply must understand the Divine Expectations set before us.

For the record, regarding our enjoyment, God did not lock us in a box. Nor did He create us as robots, so why are we making robots out of ourselves in a cycle of déjà vu or disrespecting ourselves and others?

We have Divine Dominion and Freedom, yet we lose ground because we cannot hear the Voice of God correctly. Or, we play God Almighty, trying a little bit of this and a little of that, knowing nothing about our Blueprinted Purpose. While at the same time, not knowing that JOY is one of the Fruits of the Spirit.

According to the Heavenly of Heavens, God meant for us to have JOY in us. This is what In-JOY-Ment is all about, right? Of course. However, we must know how to extract and convert the Elements of Joy, *As It Pleases God*, by truly knowing who we are and why, attuning ourselves with the *Resonating Sounds* of the Kingdom.

Can we really attune ourselves to the Sounds of Heaven? Absolutely. It is similar to a parent knowing the sounds, tones, and inflections associated with their children. The same applies to Spiritual Beings having a human experience in the Realm of the Spirit. According to the Bible and *As It Pleases God*, "My sheep hear My voice, and I know them, and they follow Me." John 10:27.

For this reason, it behooves us to unveil our Spiritual Eyes, Ears, and Voice to ensure we do not miss the MARK or the Leading of the Spirit. More importantly, when following the Voice of God, we must stay on READY, *Spirit to Spirit*, with the Fruits of the Spirit, and behaving Christlike. Therefore, if we DO NOT get it, or we 'get got,' we cannot blame anyone. Why? We are accountable, even if we do not assume responsibility!

From the Ancient of Days until now, here is what we must know: *"All the people, from the least to the greatest, came near and said to Jeremiah the prophet, 'Please, let our petition be acceptable to you, and pray for us to the LORD your God, for all this remnant (since we are left but a few of many, as you can see), that the LORD your God may show us the way in which we should walk and the thing we should do.' Then Jeremiah the prophet said to them, 'I have heard. Indeed, I will pray to the LORD your God according to your words, and it shall be, that whatever the LORD answers you, I will declare it to you. I will keep nothing back from you.' So they said to Jeremiah, 'Let the LORD be a true and faithful witness between us, if we do not do according to everything which the LORD your God sends us by you. Whether it is pleasing or displeasing, we will obey the voice of the LORD our God to whom we send you, that it* may be well with us when we obey the voice of the LORD our God.' " Jeremiah 42:1-6.

What Displeases God?

Can you differentiate between actions that are pleasing and displeasing? Do you comprehend how your moral compass functions? Do you recognize the actions that are considered displeasing in the Eye of God? Do you understand how to seek forgiveness after displeasing Him? Do you understand the consequences of displeasing Him? In order to please God, it is only fair to understand what displeases Him, right?

The concept of displeasing God has been placed on the back burner as if it has zero meaning in real-time. But we must learn the difference between what is pleasing and displeasing in the Eye of God. Why must we know the difference as Believers? It is essential for living a fulfilling and meaningful life with self-awareness that can regulate and govern positive outcomes, and how to create a win-win when things do not go as planned.

Spiritually Speaking, pleasing actions and behaviors are those that bring happiness, contentment, and positive outcomes or challenges to build, mold, train, and make us. For example, acts of kindness, empathy, respect, and compassion contain a sweet aroma in the Eye of God, building our inner man by default.

Meanwhile, unpleasing actions and behaviors are those that bring unhappiness, discontentment, and negative outcomes. Even when it appears that we are succeeding with our debaucherous efforts, it still contains a seed designed to break us down in due season. Here are a few things that break down the human psyche by default, but not limited to such:

- ☐ Injustice and oppression.
- ☐ Arrogance and contention.

- ☐ Lack of compassion and empathy.
- ☐ Dishonesty and deceit.
- ☐ Neglecting one's responsibilities.
- ☐ Intolerance and hatred.
- ☐ Unforgiveness and revenge.
- ☐ Hatefulness and bitterness.
- ☐ Jealousy and envy.
- ☐ Coveting and competitiveness.
- ☐ Greed and ungratefulness.
- ☐ Disobedience and the blaming game.

By cultivating the understanding of what is pleasing and what is not for Divine Awareness, *As It Pleases God*, we must begin to align our character according to Kingdom Standards, putting worldliness at bay.

Why must we become knowledgeable in this area, especially when having free will? In developing humility, teachability, and obedience, we must know what displeases God and what has the potential to short-circuit our *Resonating Sound* or Abilities. Here is what we must know: Proverbs 6:16-19 says, "*These six things the Lord hates, Yes, seven are an abomination to Him.*"

- ☐ A proud look.
- ☐ A lying tongue.
- ☐ Hands that shed innocent blood.
- ☐ A heart that devises wicked plans.
- ☐ Feet that are swift in the running to evil.
- ☐ A false witness who speaks lies.
- ☐ One who sows discord among brethren.

When we behave in such a manner, it can block our prayers or reap coals upon us in ways that may create generational curses. But more importantly, we must also be cautious about a few character traits contributing to these behaviors. Listed below are a few things we need to take note of:

- ☐ Pridefulness.
- ☐ Selfishness.
- ☐ Envy.
- ☐ Jealousy.
- ☐ Greed.
- ☐ Coveting.
- ☐ Lust of the Eye.
- ☐ Lust of the Flesh.
- ☐ Slothfulness.
- ☐ Disrespectfulness.
- ☐ Revengeful Anger.
- ☐ Disobedience.
- ☐ Cruelty.
- ☐ Hatefulness.

Remember, we all appear right in our own eyes, so we must do a check-up from the neck up often. Why? It is challenging to see ourselves without looking through an outside source. For example, the only way to see our outside appearance is to use a mirror, right? Being that we are all subjected to error, the same applies to our inner appearance as well; we must use a *Spiritual Mirror* to contend with *The Natural Elements* of life.

The Natural Elements

Do you know what is natural? Do you enjoy the natural elements of living life? Do you recognize the natural things that benefit you? In what ways do you incorporate natural elements into your home and work environment? Are you ready to cultivate a deeper appreciation for the beauty of the natural world? Are you prepared to learn from the wisdom of the natural world to spark your creativity?

According to the Heavenly of Heavens, we are most often tested through our bodies and the land we inhabit. As human beings, we are intricately connected to the environment around us, even if we are in denial. Our bodies and the land we inhabit are deeply intertwined, leading to numerous experiences that shape our lives.

Our DNA is programmed to repair itself in two fundamental ways: through life or death. Therefore, we must prepare ourselves, as well as our culture, to live. If not, it will naturally begin to break down to remove or eliminate us. Whether through illness, injury, or the natural aging process, we will be tested regarding our choice of the two.

Why are we tested? To challenge or determine our strength, resilience, interconnectedness, and ability to adapt to responsibility and relationships.

In the Bible, it speaks about training up a child in the way that they should go, and when they grow old, they will never depart from it. Most often, we think that scripture is only referring to a child; however, in my opinion, it is applicable to every area of our lives. For this reason, we need to bring the Natural Elements of Nature, Prayer, and the Spirit to the forefront. Here is the breakdown of a few, but not limited to such:

THE NATURAL ELEMENTS OF NATURE:

- ☐ Sunlight
- ☐ Water.
- ☐ Oxygen.
- ☐ Wind.
- ☐ Rain.
- ☐ Trees.
- ☐ Pollination.

- ☐ Seasons.
- ☐ Cycles.
- ☐ Soil and Other Nutrients.
- ☐ Photosynthesis.
- ☐ Use of Herbs, Vegetables, and Fruits.
- ☐ Biodiversity.
- ☐ Waste Elimination or Decomposition.

THE NATURAL ELEMENTS OF PRAYER:

- ☐ Worshipping.
- ☐ The Word of God.
- ☐ Repenting of Sin.
- ☐ Meditation.
- ☐ Forgiving.
- ☐ Fasting.
- ☐ Faith.
- ☐ Clarity.
- ☐ Connection.
- ☐ Petitioning.
- ☐ Confession.
- ☐ Thanksgiving.
- ☐ Supplication.
- ☐ Intercession.
- ☐ Surrender.
- ☐ Hope.
- ☐ Praise.
- ☐ Guidance.
- ☐ Trust.
- ☐ Testimony.

THE NATURAL KEYS OF THE SPIRIT:

- ☐ Love.
- ☐ Joy.
- ☐ Peace.
- ☐ Patience.
- ☐ Kindness.
- ☐ Goodness.
- ☐ Gentleness.
- ☐ Faithfulness.
- ☐ Wisdom.
- ☐ Instincts.
- ☐ Favor.
- ☐ Insight.
- ☐ Direction.
- ☐ Discernment.
- ☐ Illumination.
- ☐ Self-Control.
- ☐ Protection.

What is the purpose of knowing this information? Unfortunately, we tend to forget how BLESSED we are and how God prepared everything for us. But more importantly, the moment we begin to master or get an understanding of the Divine Process, we are better able to help and respect others who do not know or understand the value of who we are and why.

Why do we need to prove ourselves to others? It is not a matter of proving. It is a matter of BEING! Simply put, if we respect the Divine System, it will respect us with the pleasantries of harmony. Without it, we have chaos. However, we cannot respect something we ignore or do not understand.

It is through the testing phases of our lives that our level of commitment shows up to bail us out. However, if we have not invested in the building of our inner self, we may crash and burn in our most eminent time of need. No, I do not wish doom and gloom on anyone, but this is a reality check—there is a time and a season for everything under the sun. Therefore, in our time of harvest, we must store up for our time of famine, for that is inevitable according to the Cycle of Life.

I certainly am a big believer in Divine Destiny because I am living proof of it. Many different paths will get us to our destination, and we must choose one. We can take the long way, the short way, the right way, or the wrong way! It is our free-willed choice.

In my opinion, every move we make in life must be well calculated, or it may work against us. I am not saying that we must overthink issues, circumstances, or events that take place in our lives. I am saying that we must think through them to ensure distractions are kept to a bare minimum. When we make decisions with this principle in mind, it will ensure we do not fall victim to instant gratification or pleasure that leads us in the wrong direction or violates our conscience.

As we look back over our lives, where we are now is a byproduct of the choices that we have made. Nothing will change unless we do, or nothing will change unless we begin to invest in ourselves. So, with that being said, please pay it forward with the right attitude while investing in your inner self.

Always remember, what is inside of you will show up when you are squeezed to the max. From me to you, never stop learning. You are an open book that is bound to be read at some point in time, so let us get rid of the auto-assumptions and grab hold of the *Benefits of Pleasing God*. Do we really get benefits? Absolutely! Here is the Spiritual Seal: *"Every good gift and every perfect gift is from above, and comes down from the Father of lights, with whom there is no variation or shadow of turning."* James 1:17.

Benefits of Pleasing God

In our fast-paced and ever-changing world, it is easy to overlook the *Benefits of Pleasing God* and the Divine Source of everything.

More importantly, the *Benefits of the Kingdom* are not forced upon us or force-fed. We must want them for ourselves because we all have a free will right to desire power, money, sex, status, fame, and fortune as the result of our desire and willingness to seek, obtain, and embrace them with or without God Almighty. Unfortunately, with this approach, we may witness a slew of rotten fruits all over the place. Still, we have the right to want what we want, how we want it, where we want it, and with whom we desire it. Here is what we must know: *"For you, brethren, have been called to liberty; only do not use liberty as an opportunity for the flesh, but through love serve one another."* Galatians 5:13.

On the other hand, for the *Benefits of the Kingdom*, we must use the Fruits of the Spirit, become a work-in-progress, and engage in acts of kindness, compassion, and self-reflection. Why should we use this approach for the *Benefits of the Kingdom*? Once again, we have free will to use them or not. Secondly, there are no Spiritual Laws when using the Fruits of the Spirit, *As It Pleases God*. Really? Yes, really! *"But the fruit of the Spirit is love, joy, peace, longsuffering, kindness, goodness, faithfulness, gentleness, self-control. Against such there is no law."* Galatians 5:22-23. But when using them correctly, they contain a natural Spiritual Compass guiding us.

However, there are Spiritual Laws against the misuse, abuse, or manipulation of Spiritual Fruits. How is this possible, especially when we have free will? Our free will does not prevent our flesh from turning on us! Nor does it prevent us from turning on ourselves. Blasphemy, right? Wrong! Here is what we must know: *"I say then: Walk in the Spirit, and you shall not fulfill the lust of the flesh. For the flesh lusts against the Spirit, and the*

Spirit against the flesh; and these are contrary to one another, so that you do not do the things that you wish." Galatians 5:16-17.

In all simplicity, we must have self-control. Without it, it will have a field day with the psyche as it creates a warring effect on our Spiritual Compass, Conscience, Instincts, or Discernment. Often enough, we desire the Benefits of the Kingdom without self-control, only to enter a battle from within that we have no clue how to contend. Please allow me to Spiritually Align: *"Where do wars and fights come from among you? Do they not come from your desires for pleasure that war in your members? You lust and do not have. You murder and covet and cannot obtain. You fight and war. You ask and do not receive, because you ask amiss, that you may spend it on your pleasures."* James 4:1-3.

Regardless of whether we operate *As It Pleases God* or to please ourselves, the ambiguities in our ambitions determine the pleasantness or disgust in how we feel, think, believe, or behave. Unbeknown to most, the way we perceive or process life is hidden in knowing the *Benefits of God*, the Kingdom, and worldliness. By understanding the differences, we can better put people, places, and things into their proper perspective. We cannot ignore God, the Kingdom, and worldliness as if they do not exist, or it will downplay our Heavenly Benefits, *As It Pleases God.*

Simply put, Kingdom Benefits, or the lack thereof, are secretly GRAFTED in the way we truly feel. How? It is usually hidden underneath the superficial facades of being something or someone we are not, instead of being our authentic selves, helping others to do likewise. If we are afraid of being ourselves, how can we maximize our Predestined Benefits or Blueprint, *As It Pleases God?* We cannot, and until we come to ourselves, God will not open the Floodgates of the Kingdom to those hellbent on being a people-pleaser instead of a God-Pleaser.

Before we go any further, we should want to Please God because it is the right thing to do, especially since we did not create ourselves. However, to receive the Benefits of the Kingdom, have you taken the time to ask God Himself? Here is what Psalm 116:12-14 says about this matter, *"What shall I render to the LORD For all His benefits toward me? I will take up the cup of salvation, and call upon the name of the LORD. I will pay my vows to the LORD now in the presence of all His people."*

To take up our Spiritual Cup of Benefits, we must become a Servant of the Kingdom, feeding God's sheep and giving THANKS in all things, regardless of how it appears to the naked eye. Really? Yes, Really! So, let us align this accordingly, *"O LORD, truly I am Your servant; I am Your servant, the son of Your maidservant; You have loosed my bonds. I will offer to You the sacrifice of thanksgiving, and will call upon the name of the LORD. I will pay my vows to the LORD now in the presence of all His people, in the courts of the LORD's house, in the midst of you, O Jerusalem. Praise the LORD!"* Psalm 116:16-19.

In changing the trajectory of our lives, God Promised us the Holy Spirit, Who is indeed our Comforter in our time of need. The Holy Spirit is our personal assistant hidden in plain sight. For this reason, we must MASTER the ability to call upon Him before depending upon others to do what we may already have the *Know-How* to do. Or, better yet, relying on Him (The Holy Spirit) to answer questions, remind us of what we already have the answers to, or to send confirmation to what He is relaying to us in our *Spirit to Spirit* Conversations is the right thing to do, especially in the Eye of God. According to scripture, let us Spiritually Seal this Promise within the human psyche; it says, *"But the Helper, the Holy Spirit, whom the Father will send in My name, He will teach you all things, and bring to your remembrance all things that I said to you."* John 14:26.

What is the purpose of having a Helper? If we do not receive Divine Help the way God has designed for us to receive it, we will become lonely, feeling like an orphan among the masses. At the same time, looking for love in all the wrong places, picking up habits catering to our longings, or developing character traits that take us away from the Will of God. But amid all, there is helpful hope for us. Here is the Divine Decree, *"And I will pray the Father, and He will give you another Helper, that He may abide with you forever—the Spirit of truth, whom the world cannot receive, because it neither sees Him nor knows Him; but you know Him, for He dwells with you and will be in you. I will not leave you orphans; I will come to you."* John 14:16-18.

As we all know, having ACCESS to God is essential. Yet, we do not often know that He has a way of hiding from us to see what we will do or how we will react. What is the purpose of God going into hiding? It is designed to TEST us and our faith, determining the Spiritual Benefits or Repercussions. Here is what the Bible has to say, *"And He said: 'I will hide My face from them, I will see what their end will be, For they are a perverse generation, Children in whom is no faith.'"* Deuteronomy 32:20.

How do we know if we are beginning to fail our God-Induced tests? It will vary from person to person, situation to situation, anointing to anointing, and so on. However, we must MASTER what He hates and what provokes Him. For example, Deuteronomy 32:21 says, *"They have provoked Me to jealousy by what is not God; They have moved Me to anger by their foolish idols. But I will provoke them to jealousy by those who are not a nation; I will move them to anger by a foolish nation."*

The bottom line is that by participating in what is NOT pleasing in the Eye of God and engaging in idolatry, they are both firestarters in the Kingdom. Why? They cause corruption and debauchery in everything we do, say, and become, without realizing what is happening until we are royally yoked or soul-tied. All of which will eventually result in some form of defeat or humiliation, as if we are the victim, forgetting the previous seeds sown in and out of season. Then again, it may place cracks in our foundation, initiating instabilities within the human psyche while appearing strong.

For this reason, we should keep in mind, when in a state of outright disobedience, *"The sword shall destroy outside; there shall be terror within for the young man and virgin, the nursing child with the man of gray hairs."* Deuteronomy 32:25. What does this have to do with us? No one is exempt from inner traumas, especially when the swords of deeds and weapons of destruction are involved.

Listen, we cannot approach God sideways and expect Him to accept what we are offering. From much experience, He will become SILENT on us. Why? Indulging in what He hates is an insult to the Kingdom and what it stands for. We cannot feed God what He does not like and then expect the Heavenly Benefits to flow in and out of our lives without fail and on our terms.

As It Pleases God, if we give Him what He wants, He will give us the desires of the heart, benefiting us for the greater good. For the record, God is not complicated; we make Him appear as such because we like treading the fence, gratifying the lust of the eyes, lusts of the flesh, and indulging in the pride of life. What does this mean? The superficial images of being Heaven Sent or superior over another exhaust us, complicating our lives beyond measure. In so many words, keeping up with the Joneses keeps us stressed out, confused, and frustrated with ourselves, others, and God.

When we expect outer benefits before the inner ones, we inadvertently set ourselves up to become wishy-washy, unpredictable, and self-made. Whereas, if we kept up with God, we would find our lives taking a whole new direction with an accurate filter and testing system from the Heavenly of Heavens. When our lives are appropriately aligned with the Will of God or our Divine Blueprint, it will attract those who are in the plan and purge those who are not. For this reason, when benefiting in the Eye of God, we cannot become too emotionally attached or refuse to let go of what or who is not a part of our Divine Mission.

To capitalize on the *Benefits of Pleasing God*, we must know what moves Him to ACTION on our behalf. Listen to me and listen well: God loves the Fruits of the Spirit! All of which cannot be bought, even if we attempt to do so. Plus, if we attempt to purchase something appearing as a Fruit of the Spirit, it is only temporary or conditional. In due time, the wolf in sheep's clothing will reveal itself when provoked.

Why does God love the Fruits of the Spirit and Christlike Character? They help us become and remain Spiritually Righteous in the Eye of God, NOT in the eye of man. Here is the Spiritual Seal: *"And this I pray, that your love may abound still more and more in knowledge and all discernment, that you may approve the things that are excellent, that you may be sincere and without offense till the day of Christ, being filled with the fruits of righteousness which are by Jesus Christ, to the glory and praise of God."* Philippians 1:9-11.

The Mastering Process

According to the Heavenly of Heavens, if we Master the Fruits of the Spirit and use Christlike Character Traits, *As It Pleases God*, we will not have an issue with loving God, ourselves, and others with no strings attached.

How can the MASTERING PROCESS of our Spiritual Fruits really work on our behalf? We must first learn how to use them, *As It Pleases God*, to avoid the selective use of them. Actually, He desires CONSISTENT use without using them on our own terms selfishly. But of course, it takes practice, application, and correction from the Holy Spirit to help us become selfless in our use.

For example, the ultimate bliss of Inner Joy will become surreal to the onlookers, confounding the naysayers. Supernatural Peace brings a calmness within the human psyche that science has yet to tap into, making the issues of life become our driving force or footstool ALL THE WAY UP!

Kindness can be exhibited amid the Vicissitudes designed to cause us to lash out or get out of character. Righteousness and Goodness Mentally, Physically, Emotionally, and Spiritually carry a Cloak of Favor, putting our enemies to boot. The trustworthy Faithfulness makes us a force to be reckoned with in or out of the Kingdom. The Gentleness of the Kingdom helps us to speak the language of another, causing them to open up to us where they were previously closed. Most of all, the exhibition of Self-Control allows us to become disciplined in the areas that most would neglect correction.

What are the Spiritual Benefits associated with *The Mastering Process* of the Fruits of the Spirit and Christlike Character? It contains the Hidden Illumination of the Commandments already written on the Tablet of the Heart through the Blood of Jesus. Unbeknown to most, this is needed to keep our hands Blessed and Divinely Guided, allowing us to self-correct before God-Correction occurs. Here is what Proverbs 6:21-23 says, *"Bind them continually upon your heart; tie them around your neck. When you roam, they will lead you; when you sleep, they will keep you; and when you awake, they will speak with you. For the commandment is a lamp, and the law a light; reproofs of instruction are the way of life."*

If we plan on straddling the fence with the Benefits of God, we will create limits from the inside out. How do we change the trajectory of this? It will vary from person to person, situation to situation, culture to culture, and so on. But here are a few tips to get started:

- ☐ We must obey the Spiritual Principles, Laws, and Systems of God. *"Blessed are the undefiled in the way, who walk in the law of the LORD!"* Psalm 119:1.

- ☐ We must become willing to seek and serve God through the Power of our Faith-Based Testimonies.

"Blessed are those who keep His testimonies, who seek Him with the whole heart!" Psalm 119:2.

- [ ] We must become intentional with our Walk with God. *"They also do no iniquity; they walk in His ways."* Psalm 119:3.

- [ ] We must become adamant about following Kingdom Instructions. *"You have commanded us to keep Your precepts diligently."* Psalm 119:4.

- [ ] We must become mindful about what we do, say, become, or engage in. *"Oh, that my ways were directed To keep Your statutes!"* Psalm 119:5.

- [ ] We must pray, repent, and worship with a cheerful heart. *"I will praise You with uprightness of heart, when I learn Your righteous judgments."* Psalm 119:7.

- [ ] We must revamp the mind with the Word of God. *"I will meditate on Your precepts, and contemplate Your ways. I will delight myself in Your statutes; I will not forget Your word."* Psalm 119:15-16.

- [ ] We must own our truth. *"I have chosen the way of truth; Your judgments I have laid before me."* Psalm 119:30.

- [ ] We must become willing to walk in freedom, Mentally, Physically, and Emotionally. *"And I will walk at liberty, for I seek Your precepts."* Psalm 119:45.

- [ ] We must become willing to operate with clean hands and a pure heart. *"Let my heart be blameless regarding Your statutes, that I may not be ashamed."* Psalm 119:80.

- ☐ We must pay attention to ourselves, others, and what is going on around us. "*My eyes are awake through the night watches, that I may meditate on Your word.*" Psalm 119:148.

- ☐ We must delight ourselves in the Word of God as a hidden gem. "*I rejoice at Your word as one who finds great treasure.*" Psalm 119:162.

Although no one is perfect, as we become a work-in-progress for the Kingdom, it is always best to establish our *Spirit to Spirit* Relationship in our private place. Why? "*Jesus answered and said to him, 'If anyone loves Me, he will keep My word; and My Father will love him, and We will come to him and make Our home with him. He who does not love Me does not keep My words; and the word which you hear is not Mine but the Father's who sent Me.*'" John 14:23-24. If we love Him, we will take the time to develop the *Spirit to Spirit* Relationship He desires from us, instead of expecting the Benefits of the Kingdom without genuine love in return.

As It Pleases God, here are a few applicable scriptures to request Divine Illumination or to become adequately positioned in the Eye of God for His Benefits:

- ☐ "*Open my eyes, that I may see Wondrous things from Your law.*" Psalm 119:18.

- ☐ "*Remove from me the way of lying, and grant me Your law graciously.*" Psalm 119:29.

- ☐ "*Teach me, O LORD, the way of Your statutes, and I shall keep it to the end.*" Psalm 119:33.

- ☐ "*Give me understanding, and I shall keep Your law; indeed, I shall observe it with my whole heart.*" Psalm 119:34.

- ☐ "Make me walk in the path of Your commandments, for I delight in it." Psalm 119:35.

- ☐ "Incline my heart to Your testimonies, and not to covetousness." Psalm 119:36.

- ☐ "Turn away my eyes from looking at worthless things, and revive me in Your way." Psalm 119:37.

- ☐ "Teach me good judgment and knowledge, for I believe Your commandments." Psalm 119:66.

- ☐ "Look upon me and be merciful to me, as Your custom is toward those who love Your name." Psalm 119:132.

- ☐ "Direct my steps by Your word, and let no iniquity have dominion over me." Psalm 119:133.

- ☐ "Let Your hand become my help, for I have chosen Your precepts." Psalm 119:173.

- ☐ "Let my soul live, and it shall praise You; and let Your judgments help me." Psalm 119:175.

After reciting these scriptures, make sure documentation takes place using your *Spirit to Spirit* Journal to help keep track of the transformational process. Why must we document? It helps us keep track of what God is saying to and through us.

In addition, when documenting in the Gratitude Journal separately, it will help us keep track of our Blessings. What is the purpose of keeping up with our Blessings? We can easily forget about what God has already done for us.

So, when the enemy comes at us sideways, we have our Testimonies and Blessings documented in our Journals as a point of reflection while quoting Psalm 121:1-8. *"I will lift up my eyes to the hills—from whence comes my help? My help comes from the LORD, Who made heaven and earth. He will not allow your foot to be moved; He who keeps you will not slumber. Behold, He who keeps Israel shall neither slumber nor sleep. The LORD is your keeper; the LORD is your shade at your right hand. The sun shall not strike you by day, nor the moon by night. The LORD shall preserve you from all evil; He shall preserve your soul. The LORD shall preserve your going out and your coming in From this time forth, and even forevermore."*

When dealing with the BENEFITS of God, the goal is to avoid the mindset of bargaining or begging Him for what rightly belongs to us. We must AWAKEN from our slumbered mindsets by giving thanks in all things! As iron sharpens iron, we have what it takes—we simply need to know it! And what we do not possess, there is no need to worry, draining our Spiritual Power over people, places, and things we cannot change. Remember this: What is for us will be, and what is not for us cannot remain.

I totally understand how easy it is to fall into a state of begging and pleading with God about something or someone in times of trouble, loneliness, or frustration, only to become left in a state of regret and delusion once the dust settles. In a world that often pressures us to present a polished and perfect façade, if we proclaim that this does not happen to us, we are lying and deceiving ourselves.

Who am I to proclaim someone is lying without knowing them, right? The fact is that we are all human! Which means that struggles, temptations, and pitfalls come with our Heaven on Earth Experiences, embodied in the stories of our TESTIMONIES and HISTORY. Besides, our DNA does not lie; it has a patterned history as well. Plus, I have been in this position, standing at the crossroads of despair, playing god over my own life, operating in the Spirit of Disobedience, making a total mess, so to speak.

Nevertheless, in the cleanup process, *As It Pleased God*, I was able to Spiritually Glean this information for a time such as this. Therefore, in *The Mastering Process*, I make it my business to prevent others from making the same mistakes as I once did. In addition, I also provide relevant roadmaps, charts, and lists with an understanding from a Divine Perspective.

I did not have this information amid my hiccups in life, but now that we have it documented, *As It Pleases God*, we should use it to our benefit and for the greater good. Although mistakes can sometimes be our greatest teacher, certain wisdom and lessons can be gleaned from others if we pay attention and follow instructions.

When operating to please ourselves selfishly or fleshly, we lose a few Kingdom Benefits and Divine Access, similar to the Adam and Eve Experience, even if we pretend to have it going on. Simply put, their experience mirrors the contemporary struggle we are facing today, battling with obedience and commitment to God Almighty, *As It Pleases Him*.

Amid all, according to Ephesians 1:3, first and foremost, here is what we should quote back to God, *Spirit to Spirit*, over whatever or whomever to Spiritually Seal our BENEFITS: "*Blessed be the God and Father of our Lord Jesus Christ, who has blessed us with every spiritual blessing in the heavenly places in Christ.*"

Secondly, according to Ephesians 1:4, here is the Spiritual Contingency Clause hidden in plain sight: "*Just as He chose us in Him before the foundation of the world, that we should be holy and without blame before Him in love.*"

Today, my friend, straighten your Spiritual Crown and step up to the plate to POSSESS the Promises and the Benefits of the Kingdom while adjusting your *Spiritual Mirror*.

Chapter 4
Spiritual Mirror

When reflecting on our lives, we must often evaluate ourselves by God's Divine Principles and Standards to comprehend where we are, where we are going, and where we have been. Ignoring any of the three could erect a roadblock or fog up our *Spiritual Mirror*, preventing an understanding from occurring, *As It Pleases God*. Plus, it allows people to get into our heads to distort the reflections of what we see or create illusions of what we desire to satiate a longing.

What is a *Spiritual Mirror*? It is the reflection and correction of our Christlike Character and the echoes of our Fruits of the Spirit, showing us ourselves, AS IS. Above and beyond the call of duty, it also consists of our ONENESS with the Holy Spirit. Really? Yes, really! This ONENESS helps us heed the Holy Spirit's leading or correction.

What makes having a *Spiritual Mirror* so important in the Eye of God? Without chastisement, we become selfish, disobedient, disrespectful, or unruly by default, creating a sense of normality that contradicts Christlike Character to the 10th degree. Why the 10th degree? Is it that serious? Yes, this is serious when it comes down to our Spirituality in the Eye of God.

According to the Heavenly of Heavens, God uses people like us to accomplish His wondrous work in Earthen Vessels. Thus, when missing our Spiritual Timing or Mark, or when we do not Spiritually See people, places, and things correctly, it can put us in hot water with God Almighty, making the Mind, Body, and Soul foggy. For example, it is like having a brain fog out of nowhere or experiencing a brain freeze from something icy cold. If left in this state too long, we will seek comfort elsewhere as our vision becomes distorted over time.

Nevertheless, the comfort sought when we get foggy will vary from person to person, situation to situation, conditioning to conditioning, bias to bias, trauma to trauma, and so on. So, instead of running to alcohol, cigarettes, pills, food, or sex for comfort, why not run to repenting, fasting, and prayer for solutions, or '*The 24-Hour Anointing*'?

Why 24 hours when dealing with our *Spiritual Mirrors*? The Bible says clearly that the evening and the morning were the first day. Therefore, how we REFLECT daily matters to Him. More importantly, what we RELEASE matters most. If we lay down our burdens in the evening and begin our mornings fresh, this is our 24 hours for change or new opportunities for a proposed cycle, transitioning from day to day. Is it not from the evening and the morning 12 hours? Of course, it may appear like 12 hours when looking at it from a human perspective. Unfortunately, this is how we 'get got' with the issues of life.

From a Spiritual Perspective, we RELEASE our issues in the evening, giving God to the following evening to fulfill the ACTIONS we put in motion during the morning and afternoon. To complete the entire cycle in the evening, it behooves us to keep our ACTIONS positive, productive, and fruitful, *As It Pleases God*. Why? It makes the releasing process easier without Spiritual Yokes, Bondage, and Generational Curses resisting our growth or tilling process. Nonetheless, whatever we have going on in the background, if the days can change in 24 hours, so can we, right? Of course, we simply need to know what is expected of us in the Eye of God with our personalized time.

Listen, if our days run together without a FRESH ANOINTING, it indicates we are not releasing correctly. Then again, we could be toxic or reflecting on the negative, so it behooves us to check our thoughts, words, or inner chatter to determine the breach.

Regarding our *Spiritual Mirror*, remember that everyone is different, having various Divine Timings, Seasons, Cycles, Vicissitudes, and Spiritual Training or Classrooms. Hence, we need the Holy Spirit and cover ourselves with the Blood of Jesus to usher in what we NEED, *As It Pleases God*. We cannot consider what we think we need, want, or desire to please ourselves or those around us. We must add Him into our equational efforts for Divine Assistance. Once again, here is the Spiritual Seal for Divine Leverage: *"But the Helper, the Holy Spirit, whom the Father will send in My name, He will teach you all things, and bring to your remembrance all things that I said to you."* John 14:26.

Why must we include the Holy Trinity in our dealings, especially when it is just a *Spiritual Mirror*? In doing the do, whatever it may or may not be, a *Spiritual Mirror* contains Spiritual Seals, unlike a manufactured one. Theoretically, it SEALS us like a fusional graft into the Kingdom with Divine Teachings, Understanding, and Wisdom.

Then again, failing to use a *Spiritual Mirror* can graft or prune us out of having a Spiritual Seal. Is this fair? Absolutely! We must learn, obey, grow, overcome, and pursue. If not, our immaturity will make us septic, weak, and vulnerable. Is this Biblical? I would have it no other way, especially when dealing with Spiritual Seals as such. But let us deal with it in two parts:

- ☐ First Spiritual Seal: *"And if some of the branches were broken off, and you, being a wild olive tree, were grafted in among them, and with them became a partaker of the root and fatness of the olive tree, do not boast against the branches. But if you do boast, remember that you do not support the root, but the root supports you. You will say then, 'Branches were broken off that I might be grafted in.' "* Romans 11:17-19.

- ☐ Second Spiritual Seal: *"And they also, if they do not continue in unbelief, will be grafted in, for God is able to graft them in again. For if you were cut out of the olive tree which is wild by nature, and were grafted contrary to nature into a cultivated olive tree, how much more will these, who are natural branches, be grafted into their own olive tree? For I do not desire, brethren, that you should be ignorant of this mystery, lest you should be wise in your own opinion, that blindness in part has happened to Israel until the fullness of the Gentiles has come in."* Romans 11:23-25.

We all have equal rights to our *Spiritual Mirror*. No one is better than the next because we all have our Predestined Blueprint. Plus, whether we get it right, now or later, God created time for us; He will wait until we are ready. Why would He wait on us? *"For the gifts and the calling of God are irrevocable."* Romans 11:29.

Even though we renege on the Divine Agreement after making it to the Earthly Realm, He does not! Eventually, with the Cycle and Vicissitudes of Life, we will get it right. Really? Yes, really. The Cycle of Déjà vu does not have a time frame; it is based on the frameable lessons attached. Actually, it is set on repeat, becoming more challenging with each failed lesson, doing what it is designed to do. For this reason, it is best to have a *Spirit to Spirit* Relationship to download the DETAILS of the Divine Agreement instead of banking on trial and error.

Why do we need the Holy Spirit, especially when God created us a little lower than Angels to deal with our own issues? Let me counteract this question with another one, *"For what man knows the things of a man except the spirit of the man which is in him? Even so no one knows the things of God except the Spirit of God."* 1 Corinthians 2:11. The bottom line is that He keeps us from becoming shady, lying to ourselves about our condition, or playing pretend to cover up or mask up.

The Holy Spirit is not for Himself but for us, period. He is our lifetime GUARANTEE from God, the Manufacturer. Is He really with us for a lifetime? I will let the scriptures answer this question: *"And I will pray the Father, and He will give you another Helper, that He may abide with you forever."* John 14:16. If we do not KNOW this, we cannot redeem ourselves appropriately.

Why must we avoid becoming shady amid redemption in the Eye of God, especially when *Pleasing Him*? Having a high level of shady characteristics or corrupt character is a hidden weapon of mass destruction, negatively dividing the psyche without us realizing its impact. By not using a *Spiritual Mirror* to counteract our shadiness, instead of helping ourselves, we pierce oozing, hidden, or unresolved triggers. Really? Yes, really! When breathing the Breath of Life, no one is exempt from triggers; however, we must know what they are and what to do about them.

How does our psyche become divided, especially when having it all together? According to the Heavenly of Heavens, having too many negative, unresolved, or hidden triggers will keep our personality split, making us oblivious to the great divide.

In the society of the great divide, we are often conditioned to DENY our slated emotions, attitudes, or masks. Even if it is apparent that we are switching from person to person from within, amid a single encounter, we think this behavior is okay. Well, in the Eye of God, it is not. Having to play clean up after becoming an emotional wreck, breaking down mentally, or allowing our anger to go through the roof is unacceptable. Not attempting to interject Spiritual Help or taking a Mental Break will cause justification, rationalizing, and excuses to be used as a copout.

If we do not believe this is happening, we must check our thoughts, words, or emotions. They can go from 0 to 100 quickly, causing us to lose control from the inside out with a *Spiritual Mirror* nowhere in sight, as justification, rationalizing, and excuses become proactively plausible. For this reason, we need SELF-CONTROL to prevent our thoughts, words, and emotions from making it into reality, period.

When it is all said and done, God is looking for CONSISTENCY from within. To do so, we must stop lying to the psyche and become ONE in Him, using this Spiritual Seal: *"But you shall receive power when the Holy Spirit has come upon you; and you shall be witnesses to Me in Jerusalem, and in all Judea and Samaria, and to the end of the earth."* Acts 1:8.

Spiritually Investing

As we meander through life, we tend to forget about the people, places, and things contributing to where we are today, when it only takes a fraction of a second to become grateful. When we are privileged to have something or someone, it is in our nature to seek more outside of the Will of God without realizing it. For this reason, we must add Him into the Spiritual Equation to ensure our Kingdom Capital does not become liabilities in Earthen Vessels.

As we go deeper into the Spirit of Gratefulness, pleasing God is a free-will choice. Contrary to what most would think, He will not force Himself on us or bogart our lives, even if we find ourselves blaming Him for our decisions, having a pity party, or indulging in temper tantrums.

Before we go any further, regardless of our choices, to keep Divine Favor flowing, it is always best to Honor and Respect the SOURCE of our being. It does not matter whether we agree with them or understand their method of operation or reasoning; we must keep our hands clean in this area. Why is this so important in Kingdom Formality? When we are GRATEFUL to the Life-Giver (God and our Parents), we graft in long LIFE and PEACE.

Whereas, on the other hand, disrespectfulness shortens our life span from the inside out, zapping our PEACE. According to scripture, it says, *"Honor your father and your mother, as the LORD your God has commanded you, that your days may be long, and that it may be well with you in the land which the LORD your God is giving you."* Deuteronomy 5:16.

The free will exchange of Respectfulness in or out of the Kingdom of God is real, nor should it be taken lightly. Why? There is a contingency Clause hidden in plain sight in Deuteronomy 5:16 (*that it may be WELL with you in the land which the LORD your God is GIVING you*). As a word to the Wise, whenever we lack Peace, it is best to look for the areas of disrespectfulness, ungratefulness, or pompousness. What makes this so important? God frowns upon the overlooked, selfish, or undealt with self-inflicted initiations of the heart.

According to the Heavenly of Heavens, when it comes down to possessing the Promises of the Kingdom, we must prioritize God and His Business. What is the purpose of doing so? In the Kingdom, Divine Order and the Will of God matter! If we place ourselves before God or exclude Him from the equation for instant gratification, we are out of order, period. As a result, our lives will reflect likewise, regardless of how well we think we have it together or how anointed we are.

Unbeknown to most, the disorder is always reflected in our fruits, character, attitude, habits, and lusts, masked under superficial layers or masks of our choice. How do we pinpoint the erring process? Red flags should always alert us when there is a lack of humility, bragging, disobedience, selfishness, or recklessness in the camp, distorting our perception.

On the other hand, if we place others before God, here again, we are out of order as well. Are we not supposed to love our neighbor? Absolutely! Yet, there is order in loving our neighbor as well. According to scripture, *'Love your neighbor as you love thyself.'* Matthew 19:19. It is imperative to love ourselves first to love others properly.

Why must we love ourselves first? If we lack love for ourselves, jealousy, envy, pride, coveting, competitiveness, insecurity, and pompousness will spoil our fruits and character. All of this contributes to undercover or underhanded people-pleasing, fakeness, pretense, debauchery, showboating, and disrespectfulness.

What is Kingdom Order? It is placing God first, self next, and then others. Really? Yes, really! When living our lives, *As It Pleases God* allows the Holy Spirit and the Blood of Jesus to cover us while in a Spiritual Classroom of Kingdom Development. More importantly, placing God first helps us love Him as He loves us, then sharing it abroad without imposing offenses on others. In addition, it also keeps us from setting superficial or selfish conditions with ourselves and others, having nothing to do with God. What does this mean? It is when we use the Word of God to manipulate and control others for selfish gain, lustful desires, discredit other Believers, or make God a liar.

Truly loving God in the good and the bad teaches us how to endure and love ourselves while allowing us to deal with and understand our Divine Blueprint and Genetic Makeup. Obtaining this type of understanding helps us manifest the training, lessons, regrafting, cleansings, or unyoking needed to possess the Promises of God.

Once we understand who we are and why, we can love our neighbor, putting aside our quirks, biases, and cultural differences and doing what we are called to do. What if we are rejected? Listen, regardless of whether or not we are rejected, we are called to do our due diligence in the Spirit of Excellence.

We are designed to make an impactful difference, and if we are hateful, rude, arrogant, or disrespectful, the Promises of God can pass us by. How is this possible when the fight is fixed? If we do not recognize the fight, we are not equipped, or we are defeated in it, then Spiritual Blindness, Deafness, and Muteness will become our portion until we come to ourselves.

We are created in the Image of God, and if we downplay our Blueprint, Birthright, or His Promises, forfeiture is placed on the horizon. What does this mean? We are at risk of losing what rightly belongs to us, especially if we do not step up our game. How is this a game? If we do not make the right moves, move slowly, meander unwisely, or become pompous, we subject ourselves to befalling the elements of defeat.

Frankly, no one in their right mind wants to fall short, especially when they can stand tall in the Eye of God. For this reason, we must become equipped with the Spiritual Tools to contend with the enemy's wiles. How do we go about doing so? We must stay in the *'As It Pleases God'* Realm of the Spirit or under His Wing. Here is what Psalm 91:1-4 shares with us: *"He who dwells in the secret place of the Most High Shall abide under the shadow of the Almighty. I will say of the LORD, 'He is my refuge and my fortress; My God, in Him I will trust.' Surely He shall deliver you from the snare of the fowler and from the perilous pestilence. He shall cover you with His feathers, and under His wings you shall take refuge; His truth shall be your shield and buckler."*

One of the most overlooked commodities is the inability to invest in ourselves, *As It Pleases God*. Then again, according to the Heavenly of Heavens, the obliviousness associated with *Spiritually Investing* in our Gifts, Calling, Talents, Creativity, or Divine Blueprint has placed us in the hot seat with God.

Why would we be in the hot seat, especially when we are clueless about what we need to do? Cluelessness does not give us an excuse for not trying or not becoming a work-in-progress. Actually, it distorts our self-discovery efforts by not seeing ourselves, our fruits, and our character traits clearly.

Unbeknown to most, disobedience leads to recklessness, pompousness, and a stiff neck, along with the squandering of what is designed to BLESS us to become a BLESSING while providing Spiritual Provisions for all involved. On the other hand, we are quick to invest in outward appearances without involving God in the equation, especially when He is the Creator of it all. What an insult, right? How would you feel if you created something for someone, and once they got up on their feet, they booted you out, forgot about you, or seemingly spat in your face? Regardless of how Spiritually Grounded you are, it could leave a bad taste in your mouth, especially if you are NOT doing whatever with whomever for the right reasons.

Indeed, ungratefulness has tainted the human race without us giving it a second thought. Yet, for this very reason, *As It Pleases God*, He shows Divine Favor to those who are GRATEFUL and who show RESPECT for His Divine Creation, as well as their Divine Blueprint. How do we make this make sense? Everything has a Divine Purpose for being here, contributing to the Cycle of Life, regardless of whether we understand it or not. Furthermore, in all due respect, if we have not taken the time to understand or *Spiritually Invest* in our WHY, then why are we disrespecting the WHY of another or attempting to circumvent it?

Here again, amid all, you must ask yourself a few questions, but not limited to such:

- ☐ Are you *Spiritually Investing* in regrafting yourself?
- ☐ Are you *Spiritually Investing* in having a Positive Mindset?
- ☐ Are you *Spiritually Investing* in your Spiritual Temple?
- ☐ Are you *Spiritually Investing* in your *Spirit to Spirit* Relations?
- ☐ Are you *Spiritually Investing* in your Christlike Character Traits or People Skills?
- ☐ Are you *Spiritually Investing* in your Spiritual Fruits?
- ☐ Are you *Spiritually Investing* in your Divine Blueprint?
- ☐ Are you *Spiritually Investing* in your Dreams, Calling, Talents, Creativity, and Desires?

Who wants to know about our *Spiritual Investments*? YOU need to know! According to the Heavenly of Heavens, if one has answered 'No' to any one of these questions, there is still HOPE.

As long as we are breathing the Breath of Life, we have another opportunity to get it right in the Eye of God. Amid doing so, we must equip ourselves with Spiritual Tools, preventing unnecessary do-overs that we can get right the first time around.

As life would have it, we are quick to invest in the worldly people, places, and things leading us away from the Kingdom instead of toward it! So, what do we do? We must redirect the Mind, Body, Soul, and Spirit toward Kingdom Standards and Principles, doing a clean sweep of all the known and unknown worldliness, negativity, and debauchery.

Here is the deal: Our *Spiritual Investments* determine whether we are a Profitable or Unprofitable Servant in the Kingdom. Although we can go through the motions, appearing to be one of the two. Still, our Spiritual Fruits and Character Traits reveal the truth, regardless of whether we pay attention or not.

Listen, overlooking our Spiritual Fruits and neglecting to exhibit Christlike Character Traits can prevent us from *Spiritually Investing* in ourselves, people, places, and things as we should. Why is this the case? It is due to our hidden, overlooked, or denied biases. In addition, it can also be a result of our cultural differences, limiting beliefs, selfishness, jealousy, envy, covetousness, greed, pride, or competitiveness. Even if we sugarcoat the truth, it does not negate the underlying root of whatever, with whomever, or our real WHY.

According to the Heavenly of Heavens, with our *Spiritual Investments*, we exhibit a form of Godliness, but not the Godliness from the Kingdom of Heaven. What is the difference? If our Godliness is dedicated to destroying, breaking down, hurting, or traumatizing others, we must rethink WHAT we are doing and WHY.

When we find ourselves negatively repeating or mirroring how we were treated or traumatized, making others feel the same way we secretly feel without correcting this form of behavior, we cannot lay this at the doorpost of the Kingdom. Why not, especially when doing or giving our best as Believers? If we think being nasty, rude, violent, disrespectful, and obnoxious represents the Kingdom, then we are sadly mistaken, regardless of the mask that we convey in the presence of others.

In the Kingdom, we deal with Righteousness, not unrighteousness! For this reason, it is imperative to *Spiritually Invest* in ourselves, developing our Spiritual Fruits and Character Traits, *As It Pleases God*. Of course, this does not make us perfect; actually, it makes us a work-in-progress, being able to apologize, repent, forgive, or self-correct at the drop of a dime. What makes this so important? It helps prevent the negative festering or manifestation of debauched charactorial fruits.

Playing pretend does not get us brownie points in the Kingdom; we must put in the work for ourselves. The Fruits of the Spirit and Christlike Character Traits do not come pre-packaged on a shelf. They are already within us; we must dust them off and put them to work in our favor. More importantly, no one can do this for us; we are the best *Do-It-Yourself* Project known to man.

If we want all God has to offer us, we must do our due diligence. If not, we will settle for a portion of our Birthrights, Promises, or Blessings, especially when it takes the same amount of energy, if not more, to walk away than it would to walk toward it.

A real Champion in the Eye of God possesses the Fruits of the Spirit and exhibits Christlike Character with outright humility. However, it also helps us differentiate the wolves in sheep's clothing or when to exercise extreme caution. If we miss the Spiritual Cues naturally embedded in the Fruits of the Spirit, we can get sucker-punched or tossed around with the Vicissitudes of life easily.

All in all, we must pay attention, get out of our feelings, and tame our thoughts. If not, we can become royally played in the Game of Life. How can we get played when we are on top of our game? Whether we are at the top or bottom of our game, it is a matter of perception. The enemy can smell our weaknesses a mile away, and if we hide, deny, or overlook them, they will hang us out to dry.

As a *Spiritual Investment* into ourselves, we must adequately align everything about ourselves with the Will of God or our Divine Blueprint, covering them with the Blood of Jesus. Why is it best to remain in the Will of God and cover ourselves with the Blood of Jesus as Spiritual Atonement? We can put on the Whole Armor of God with confidence, knowing we are operating with clean hands and a pure, repentant heart.

Doing so prevents the enemy from using our secrets as an uppercut to knock the breath out of us or provide a breeding ground for compromise.

On the other hand, if we are out of Divine Purpose, in denial, or contradicting the reason for our being, then we must ask, 'Are we really on top of our game?' 'Were we positioned by luck?' 'Are we riding on God's grace and mercy?' Or, 'Are we playing ourselves short?' Although God loves us all, *"For He makes His sun rise on the evil and on the good, and sends rain on the just and on the unjust."* Matthew 5:45. However, for those who listen, understand, learn, and obey the Will and Word of God, *As It Pleases Him*, their Spiritual Eyes become open to what the Spiritually Blind cannot see or comprehend. Plus, it helps us to establish ONE MIND with the Kingdom of Heaven, ensuring we are not intentionally dividing ourselves and others with selfish ambitions.

Here is what Philippians 2:1-5 says: *"Therefore if there is any consolation in Christ, if any comfort of love, if any fellowship of the Spirit, if any affection and mercy, fulfill my joy by being like-minded, having the same love, being of one accord, of one mind. Let nothing be done through selfish ambition or conceit, but in lowliness of mind let each esteem others better than himself. Let each of you look out not only for his own interests, but also for the interests of others. Let this mind be in you, which was also in Christ Jesus."*

Now, the question is, how do we become like-minded? We must *Spiritually Invest* in ourselves using the Fruits of the Spirit as a formal guide to consciously gauge what we are doing and why. When CAPITALIZING on the Fruits of the Spirit, they help us in every area without fail, creating a Cycle of Reciprocity with everyone we encounter, even if nothing is mentioned, it goes unnoticed, or others downplay it. Really? Yes, really. It is in our nature to remember how people made us feel, and if we use the Fruits of the Spirit, it UNVEILS the truth in the Eye of God, even when those around us are forming lies against us.

Personally, when using the Fruits of the Spirit and Christlike Character Traits, *As It Pleases God*, they create a worry-free environment, giving me the leverage to approach people, places, and things with a Righteous Spirit. While, at the same time, granting me the Spiritual Authority from the Heavenly of Heavens to invite the Holy Spirit to speak the language of another, positively.

Why would we need permission to speak the Spiritual Language of another? It creates a common ground of relatability to meet people where they are, where they are going, or where they have been, ensuring they do not develop a deaf ear to us, even if they pretend to do so. Listen, each person has their own unique experiences, beliefs, traumas, biases, and practices, making them who they are and establishing their uniqueness. So, we as a people must develop respect in order to develop connection, build trust, and bridge gaps, *As It Pleases God*.

On the flip side of the coin, failing to seek permission on behalf of the Heavenly of Heavens while conveying disrespect or insensitivity, this oversight will cause visible or invisible barriers to form. When we approach people, places, things, events, and situations without respect, consent, or mindfulness, it often manifests as negative consequences or conjectures, real or imagined. All of which leads to debauchery, chaos, confusion, misunderstanding, jealousy, envy, pride, contention, greed, competitiveness, and detrimental outcomes that we often deny. As a ripple effect of lying to ourselves, we develop fake connections that do not last, or we grapple with insensitivities that compel us to wear masks, overlooking what is taking place within our psyche.

When *Spiritually Investing* in ourselves and others, the goal is to seek understanding, connection, and meaning, with an authentic heart and mind posture, *As It Pleases God*. When we seek to understand God first, ourselves next, and those around us, we foster a relational climate of empathy, mercy, love, and compassion. In the Eye of God, this approach creates bonds that transcend superficial interactions, surface-level connections, and quick judgments. With this profound shift, we can ground ourselves in a source of Unconditional Love and Divine Wisdom for the Greater Good of all mankind to uplift and unite, *As It Pleases Him*.

For me, my *Spiritual Investments* help my natural talents collide with my Spiritual Ones, making me Divinely Creative with an impact on those needing what God has BLESSED me to offer. In addition, it also helps me to become appropriately equipped with the Spiritual Tools, Divine Wisdom, and the Spiritual Know-How to *Feed His Sheep*. And you are no different...Let's talk about it in the next chapter.

CHAPTER 5
ALL ONE

When expounding on being *All One* with the Holy Trinity, we must understand we are Spiritual Beings having a human experience. In addition, we must also know that we are trapped in time, with senses, emotions, and thoughts to govern the SEEDS and CYCLES set in motion by, through, and for us. What is the purpose of knowing this? From a Spiritual Perspective, we must know who we are in the Eye of God to streamline or download His Divine Perspectives. If not, we will equate ours with His, causing our Spiritual Antennas to become warped with bad, mixed, or wrong signals. Then again, we may operate in Spiritual Error or Omission without knowing it, subjecting ourselves to mediocrity and knowing nothing about our Predestined Blueprint.

How can Believers not know what they are born to do? Unfortunately, it has become a plagueable deficit for the Kingdom of God, making us easy targets for the enemy's wiles. With all due respect, with a little money, power, fame, and sex, off we go, forgetting about the Kingdom of God until we stub our toes.

How is this a plagueable deficit, especially when we have more Believers than ever? We are not adequately trained to use our Gifts, Calling, Talents, Creativity, or Purpose, *As It*

Pleases God. As a result of our unsurety or wavering piety, we fall into a system of idolatry, praising others for what they do. While at the same time, not giving a rat's tail about what we must do to align with our Predestined Blueprint. Who am I to judge someone's Spiritual Gifts, right? No judgment intended; my job is to extract, convert, redirect, or unveil, *As It Pleases God.*

My Spiritual Journey into MASTERING began at five years old, without me realizing my Grandmother was molding my Creative Genius from within. For this reason, I do not settle for excuses because she used natural elements, nature, junk, and tangible things using zero dollars, forcing me to create something out of nothing. Did it work? Well, here we are...judge for yourself!

According to the Heavenly of Heavens, no one is exempt from Divine Creativity, and no one is too young or old to begin. We all have Spiritual Tools and something to bring to the table; however, if we fail to document, pay attention, or become ONE, *As It Pleases God,* we tend to forget the vital DNA lineage linking us *In Him.*

What does *In Him* have to do with our ONENESS? We are ONE in Him, in or out of the Kingdom of God. Outside of Him, we become internally divided, socially biased, and easily corrupted in a worldly system.

According to the Ancient of Days, *In Him* is eulogized in our Heaven on Earth Experiences, but we have forgotten the Spiritual Protocol of the Kingdom for some reason. What does this mean? We are into ourselves, not God, *As It Pleases Him.* While simultaneously voicing what we need from Him and ignoring what He needs or requires from us.

What would cause us to forget Spiritual Instructions or Protocol? It could result from distractions, lack of understanding, unawareness on our behalf, conditioning, or outright Spiritual Neglect. Who knows, besides the Spirit of God, right? Wrong! WE KNOW!

We commonly use the cliché, 'We are all in' or 'We are all out.' In the Kingdom, we use the methodology 'We are all ONE in Christ Jesus.' If we are truly ONE, we know it. Then again, if we are not...the conscience knows as well. So, there is NO shaking and baking in the Eye of God; He knows. Yet, He patiently waits for us to awaken from our slumber or choose to become a work-in-progress, *As It Pleases Him*.

How do we become ONE *In Him*? We must AWAKEN from our slumber to develop a *Spirit to Spirit* Relationship with the Holy Trinity in total ONENESS. Scripturally, here is what we must know when Spiritually Aligning ourselves: "*For in Him we live and move and have our being, as also some of your own poets have said, 'For we are also His offspring.'*" Acts 17:28. Simply put, we are ONE with:

- ☐ Our God.
- ☐ Our Savior.
- ☐ The Holy Spirit.
- ☐ Our Mind.
- ☐ Our Body.
- ☐ Our Soul.
- ☐ Our Spirit.

With this sort of ONENESS, we can pinpoint the moment we jump the track Mentally, Physically, Emotionally, and Spiritually. What is the purpose of pinpointing our derailments? If we desire to become balanced in any area of our lives, we must become ONE from within, *As It Pleases God*, to properly become ONE with ourselves and others. If not, everything may become conditional, self-fulfilling, biased, or manipulative while appearing right in our own eyes.

How can we develop stipulations as such without knowing it? When our psyche rules us, it fights tooth and nail to prevent us from awakening from our slumber while justifying and rationalizing everything. If one does not believe this, then check the inner chatter and thoughts that are taking place. They offer valuable insight into our internal dialogues, thought patterns, and attitudes. In addition, it also provides a bird's eye view into our consciously or unconsciously harbored doubts, conflicting views, genuine feelings, fears, internal resistances, skepticism, self-limiting beliefs, and convictions.

For the reasons of the psyche, from the Adam and Eve event until now, we cannot redeem ourselves, no matter how hard we try. We need the Blood of Jesus to cover us, the Holy Spirit to guide us, the Fruits of the Spirit as a Heavenly Blueprint of Divine Expectations, and our Christlike Character to keep us in the RIGHT STANDING for our Heaven on Earth Experiences. If not, we become or live our lives topsy-turvy as if it is normal when it is not.

Then what do we do? We find ourselves ignoring the psyche by rushing from one thing to the next without taking the time to pause and reflect on the direction of our lives and where we are heading. As the psyche begins to run the show, the abnormal has become the new normal with quick fixes and instant everything, as we go to Instagram, YouTube, and TikTok for answers instead of going to the CREATOR of it all. Thus, God has a problem with this matter.

Divine Praying Power

Our *Divine Praying Power* is intricately interwoven with the transformative force of Spiritual Empowerment. In addition, it is also a Spiritual Pipeline of gratitude, appreciation, humility, and awareness that will extend a profound sense of interconnectedness and compassion, *Spirit to Spirit*, when used properly. According to the Heavenly of Heavens, it is our Divine Gateway to self-reflection, self-discovery, self-renewal, self-growth, self-repentance, self-forgiveness, and self-redemption. Is this not being selfish? No, using them *As It Pleases God* makes us SELFLESS and Kingdomly USABLE.

How do we redeem ourselves, *As It Pleases God*? By REPENTING! Really? Yes, really. What if we choose not to repent? We have free will to do so or not to. Nevertheless, there are negative consequences and repercussions for neglecting to repent. In addition, the lack of repentance perpetuates harm or trauma, leads to a breakdown in trust and strained relationships, and will cause us to turn on ourselves and others while appearing right in our own eyes.

Whereas, in the Eye of God, acknowledging one's wrongdoings, feeling genuine remorse, forgiving ourselves or others, assuming responsibility, and making amends to rectify the situation are needed to become liberated from the inside out or to initiate the healing process.

On the contrary, if bondage is our choice or we choose not to heal out of pride, stubbornness, disobedience, dullness, envy, jealousy, coveting, or a lack of understanding, we have the right to choose that as well. Still, know this: Inflicting pain and suffering on others, creating a cycle of hurt, leaving a trail of rotten fruit, or creating a path of destruction is a quick way to invoke generational curses.

What is the big deal about repenting? The deal is that unacknowledged wrongdoings can lead to feelings of guilt, shame, regret, anger, revenge, hatefulness, wayward prayers, and inner turmoil. All of these can put a damper on our *Spirit to Spirit* Relationship with our Heavenly Father.

Why would the lack of repentance hinder our *Divine Praying Powers* or Spiritual Relationships? The Holy Spirit cannot remain in our folly; thus, He must lie dormant. Is not the Holy Spirit designed to help us? Absolutely. He helps us when we make a conscious attempt to help ourselves, *As It Pleases God*.

How do we make this make sense, especially when we are encouraged to call on the Holy Spirit? We must make our best attempts to TRY to engage in righteousness. For example, we will run to God to fix our messes when we have the same opportunity, not to create them in the first place. Moreover, we have the exact same opportunity to say, 'Fix Me, Lord, Heal Me, Lord, Where Did I Go Wrong, Lord, or I REPENT, O'Lord,' and choose not to do so.

Divine Praying Power is a sensitive area of Spirituality, leaving room for much debate. So, once again, let us take it to scripture: *"Then Peter said to them, 'Repent, and let every one of you be baptized in the name of Jesus Christ for the remission of sins; and you shall receive the gift of the Holy Spirit.' "* Acts 2:38.

Here is the deal: When praying, repenting, and fasting, we must ensure we are not violating the free will of another or harboring unforgiveness. We must also ensure we are not doing them out of selfishness, hatefulness, or materialism. They must come from a place of LOVE and not evil.

According to the Heavenly of Heavens, if we VIOLATE THE WILL of another person through fasting, praying, or repenting, it is nothing more than witchcraft! Most people will not inform us about this sort of behavior, but I am not most people. For the record, this type of behavior leads to blocked prayers or prayers that backfire. So, beware of the intents of the heart when dealing with God Almighty.

Why must we become cognizant of our heart postures? They are being weighed! Scripturally, remember this: *"Every way of a man is right in his own eyes, But the LORD weighs the hearts. To do righteousness and justice is more acceptable to the LORD than sacrifice."* Proverbs 21:2-3.

Here is a secret: *As It Pleases God*, we must continually direct our prayers back to ourselves to avoid violating anyone's free will. When we bring our prayers back home to ourselves that are positive in nature, we are free from any form of ill will. Hint, hint...I do not know anyone who would intentionally curse themselves while praying. Therefore, it behooves us to keep it directed toward ourselves positively.

Why must we keep our prayers positive, especially when our enemies are ruthless? Because it helps to keep our communication channels open with our Heavenly Father, even when dealing with difficult, ruthless, or malevolent people.

What about King David's prayers in the Book of Psalms? God has given us a bird's-eye view of King David's prayers; although some may appear dark and gloomy, we must remember he had a lot of blood on his hands. So, there was a lot of purging of the conscience going on in the Book of Psalms.

More importantly, we will also see King David cleaning those prayers up in his *Spirit to Spirit* alone time with God. We DO NOT see him openly cursing his enemies, playing God Almighty. Instead, he took his qualms to his prayer closet for realignment, redirecting them back to himself, and documented them, *As It Pleased God.*

Amid King David's purging of the conscience, our Heavenly Father also provided Anointed Prophets to help him self-correct when erring. Why? To ensure he remained after God's own heart because everyone appears right in their own eyes; therefore, we need a *Spiritual Mirror* outside of our own.

Of course, we all will have negative stuff to work on or through; thus, we cannot leave it as-is. We must MASTER the ability to create a win-win or make it positive on our Spiritual Journey. The only way to truly map our growth process is to document it, putting pen to paper. For sure, it keeps the mind from going all the way to the left without knowing or pinpointing it.

Now that we have the Blood of Jesus as a Spiritual Covering, siccing God on others out of revenge, selfishness, jealousy, envy, pride, greed, anger, betrayal, frustration, or debauchery is a big no-no. Why should we NOT seek revenge through Divine Intervention? We do not know what Spirit is behind whatever or whomever. And, if we have not tested the

Spirit first, then we are out of order in the Eye of God. 1 John 4:1 says, *"Beloved, do not believe every spirit, but test the spirits, whether they are of God; because many false prophets have gone out into the world."*

Why do we need to test the Spirit? Some things are God Sent or God Allowed, and if our discernment faculties are warped, we may be engaging with God without knowing it. Thus, we will walk away with a limp similar to when Jacob wrestled with God in Genesis 32:22-32.

Do we really wrestle with God? It happens all too often, and we blame it on the enemy. How so? We fight against ourselves while denying the warring that is taking place from within, giving the enemy leverage to conduct a sneak attack. For this reason, 1 Thessalonians 5:21 tells us to: *"Test all things; hold fast what is good."*

What if the things we are testing are not good? Learn the lesson, create a win-win, and keep it moving in the Spirit of Excellence without trying to seek revenge. Sometimes, the lesson is more valuable than getting our lick back. Nor does it benefit us to sic God on people, especially when there is a lesson that we need to learn. Listen, do not get confused...a lesson learned is a BLESSING indeed. On the other hand, if the lesson is NOT learned, we must RETAKE the exam.

When dealing with *Divine Praying Power*, using God to seek vengeance or siccing Him on others when we have not taken the time to work on ourselves, *As It Pleases Him*, can create a Spiritual Taboo for us. Why would this happen? God deals with justification and unjustification. For example, if we pray for ill will against someone and we are guilty of doing the same to another, do we get a free pass for our debauchery? The answer is NO. Repentance and forgiveness must occur while making our best attempts to use the Fruits of the Spirit and behave Christlike.

Why must we be the bigger person with our prayers? We have a choice of being the selfless, bigger person or the selfish, small person. But know this: Trying to sic God on others often arises from a place of emotional turmoil, trauma, pain, anger, and hurt that perpetuate a cycle of negativity. For the record, attempting to invoke God's wrath on others can intensify feelings of anger and further entrench animosity, causing us to turn on ourselves.

What if we still engage? Doing so creates a disconnect from within the human psyche, causing the Holy Spirit to lie dormant until we awaken from our slumber. We CANNOT invoke God's wrath upon others as a means of seeking revenge, retaliation, or personal vendettas, especially with unrepented sin and rotten fruit all over the place. However, we DO have the right to cancel, reject, rebuke, and reverse the effects, protect ourselves, or denounce the Spirit behind whatever or whomever. But we DO NOT have the right to cast or forecast ill will, doom and gloom, curse, or bring judgment—That is God's JOB.

Unfortunately, this is how the best of the best get caught up in Spiritual Error due to the lack of understanding. For the record, a Spirit, good, bad, or indifferent, does not have free will. We must allow entry, this is why the Holy Spirit lays dormant until we AWAKEN Him and lays dormant when we begin to behave foolishly. Now, an UNCLEAN Spirit gets us to violate our own free will or that of another to gain entry through justification and through the neglect of using the Fruits of the Spirit. Unfortunately, they know Spiritual Laws better than we do, and it is time for us to step up our game and use the Fruits of the Spirit to FOOLPROOF ourselves.

Why is foolproofing necessary for Believers? Using God to harm or punish others when we have not taken the time to learn, grow, understand, and become a better person through compassion, forgiveness, mercy, and love will cause us to get a Spiritual Side-Eye from God.

What is the purpose of getting a Spiritual Side-Eye? Using God as a weapon for personal retribution, personal power and control, or out of bitterness and vindictiveness makes us morally questionable. We must leave judgment to God Almighty because we all have a Spiritual Right to free will, making us accountable for our own choices and actions. In the same way that they are accountable, so are we!

The final take on this matter is that our responsibility is to give it or them to God, not to become Him, control Him, use Him, prostitute Him, or tell Him what to do. If we are not controlling and taming our psyche, how do we think we can control others or tell God what to do? We cannot, especially if we know nothing about the Fruits of the Spirit or how to use them properly, and *As It Pleases Him*! Is this not a little insensitive? Maybe or maybe not, but what is more insensitive is for me to withhold the truth, allowing you to curse yourself due to the lack of understanding.

Moving in the Spirit of Excellence, *As It Pleases God*, keeps us in the right standing with Him amid our imperfections and weaknesses. Knowing what He expects from us or desiring to get through us determines the ultimate Spiritual Walk into our Divine Purpose with our Predestined Blueprint in hand.

As we work on ourselves, making our '*Better to Best*' or '*Good to Great*' transition, we must also become powerful team players to continue to grow, sow, and do more in the Kingdom. What is the purpose of doing more? We want to tap into our highest and greatest potential, so we must challenge ourselves to improve without settling for mediocrity.

The Spiritual Team

Building Kingdom Partnerships and Teams is part of the Heavenly System designed to work in unison. More importantly, it also helps us to align ourselves accordingly due to the expectations set forth.

When we are accountable for ourselves, it is easy to hide our progression or the lack thereof, whereas when others are involved, the facts are less likely to become buried. At the same time, this results in a higher level of accountability or fine-tuning on our behalf, especially when the right team is backing or connecting with us.

What if we do not have a team? Regardless of how we feel or what life has dealt us, we will always have a Spiritual Team called the Holy Trinity (The Father, Son, and Holy Spirit). Trust me, having this Spiritual Team backing us will guarantee that we will pack a powerful punch!

How do we go about applying this to our daily lives? As we lead in the Spirit of Excellence, we must be willing to bring people together, even if they are seemingly rejecting us or what we have to offer. Why do we need to make such an effort? A Kingdom divided against itself cannot stand; therefore, we must be willing to *Authentically* UNITE without being at odds with anyone, allowing bygones to be bygones.

According to the Heavenly of Heavens, the Power of Unity is a hidden treasure repeatedly overlooked by most. We often desire to unite outwardly, yet fail to understand the Spiritual Resilience in uniting inwardly first and then outwardly. Why is this important in the Eye of God? Inner Unity is predicated on knowing ourselves, Mind, Body, Soul, and Spirit. Without this understanding, we become aloof at developing UNITY while pretending to be publicly unified, yet all so divided from within.

What does our aloofness have to do with unity or becoming *All ONE*? Here is what I see when breaking a unit down: U NIT. If I spell it correctly, it would appear as 'You KNIT.' Although knitting is a great skill, it also has a hidden message for us to glean. When knitting, we cannot start outwardly; we must start inwardly. Or, we must have a starting point of origination to provide strong anchors for the next knit. If we have an anchor that is weak, insecure, or loose, our end result will reflect as such, with mangled outcomes or disappointments. Why would this happen to our knits? The anchor contained false expectations, which led to whatever, with whomever.

How do anchored knits apply to us in real life? A weak knit within the human psyche is derived from fear, shame, rejection, guilt, or any form of negativity, causing Spiritual Blindness, Deafness, or Muteness, instigating a side-eye from God. For example, a Positive Mental Mindset equates to having strong anchors in or out of the Kingdom, preventing us from self-destructing from the inside out while working on ourselves on a moment-by-moment basis.

On the other hand, a negative mindset indicates weak anchors, regardless of how well we try to sugarcoat or become eye candy. Unfortunately, they both melt when heat is applied. How can we avoid melting under pressure? We must become a solid rock, *As It Pleases God*. If we take a deep dive for a minute, rocks are not formed overnight. They, too, come from mushy or liquified stuff under molting pressure. Yet, have the potential to become Cornerstones of Greatness over time. What is the difference between sugary and hard stuff? Rocks contain the right components of solidarity, and sweet stuff becomes bitter or disdaining after the expiry date.

When *All One* with our Heavenly Father, we need to check our Self-Talk, People-Talk, and *Spirit to Spirit* Conversations. Our inner chatter determines how well we can overcome whatever we are going through or have faced. If we talk positively on the outside while speaking negatively from within, we will become wishy-washy, prideful, and all over the place while thinking we are on point and effective.

The Spiritual Platform of God has conditions, as with anything associated with POWER. In becoming rock-solid and *All One* in our *Spirit to Spirit* Relations, we must understand a few things, but not limited to such:

- ☐ We must remain consistent and humble, *As It Pleases God*, not as it pleases us.

- ☐ No one is perfect, nor will we be positive 100% of the time; therefore, it behooves us to hone in on self-correction instead of self-perfection.

- ☐ We must understand that there are many things we do not know; therefore, we must approach God with an open heart and mind.

- ☐ We will all be annoyed by something or someone, and we must remain calm and patient.

- ☐ We will all desire change, and we must follow instructions.

- ☐ We will all have challenges that we must work through or overcome.

- ☐ We will all encounter something or someone we do not like, care for, or ruffle our feathers for whatever reason; therefore, we must put on our kindest and wisest game face.

- ☐ We will all become vexed about something, provoking us to examine it thoroughly or pay close attention.

- ☐ We will all experience some form of trauma containing Spiritual Lessons or Healing. Therefore, we cannot run from it or them; we must learn while operating in the Spirit of Excellence.

- ☐ We will all have something we cannot change. God will always give us a thorn in our flesh to keep us humble.

- ☐ We will all come across something or someone we do not understand. As Kingdom Representatives, we do not want to walk around as if we do not have any Spiritual Home Training.

- ☐ We will all become exposed to the unexplainable to keep our faith where it needs to be.

- ☐ We will all experience temptation or a slippery slope to keep us compassionate, merciful, repenting, forgiving, and grateful.

From a Spiritual Perspective, staying out of other people's business allows us to focus on ourselves and our Divine Mission, *As It Pleases God*. In addition, it also helps us to stay in our own lane to avoid unwanted Spiritual Strikes.

What are Spiritual Strikes in the Eye of God? It is when God steps in with corrective measures similar to a parent-child relationship, serving as catalysts for personal growth, understanding, and an increased sense of purpose. Most often, Spiritual Correction or Chastisement occurs from our acts of disobedience, waywardness, when operating with a stiff neck, when distributing rotten or mangled fruits, when we become an opposing force to Kingdom Business, and so on. Then again, they often happen when we lose our *Spiritual Covering* for worldly synthetics that seem to appear better than what we have, hidden under what we call...UNGRATEFULNESS.

Spiritual Covering

The Hidden Power of God is within our reach; actually, it is within us, waiting for our beckoning call. The Awakening we so desire is already there; we only need to place the Spiritual

Demand on what is already Predestined. Amid doing so, it is imperative to gain the Spiritual Knowledge needed to place such a demand in the Eye of God.

Why must we gain knowledge in this area as Believers? If we are operating in unrighteousness or functioning with what is not a part of our Divine Blueprint, we will suffer setbacks and disappointments, letting us know that we are on the wrong path, we are out of order, or we are unclean.

In our Hidden Power, God has PROMISED us a Spiritual Covering or Sacrifice through the Blood of Jesus. It is through the Blood of Christ that we can stake our claim to our Divine Birthrights, Promises, and Blessings. Unbeknown to most, if we reject the Blood of Christ, there will still be a sacrifice made amid whatever or whomever, and we may not be able to choose the area or person on the bargaining table. *As It Pleases God*, it behooves us to freely choose the Blood of Jesus to ensure we keep our Bloodline safe, secured, Blessed, and Anointed.

In aligning this accordingly, this is similar to Noah building the Ark, covering it with pitch, a natural tar-like substance, in Genesis 6:14 as a Spiritual Seal from the Heavenly of Heavens. It says, *"Make yourself an ark of gopherwood; make rooms in the ark, and cover it inside and outside with pitch."* Noah was briefed on the *What* and *Why*, and then he was given specific instructions on the *How-To* and *Know-How* to carry out his Divine Mission, *As It Pleased God*.

Based upon the Divine Grace bestowed upon Noah, it positioned him to hear, see, and do what most could not in the Eye of God. Here is the key: *"Thus Noah did; according to all that God commanded him, so he did."* Genesis 6:22. What does this mean for us? Obedience and Righteousness in the Eye of God usher in more of what the Kingdom offers freely. What is it? Was it manna, the food from Heaven? It was SPECIFIC INSTRUCTIONS that most were not privy to receiving. In aligning this, in Genesis 7:1, *"Then the LORD said to Noah, Come* into the ark, you and all your household, because I have seen that you are righteous before Me in this generation."

In today's day and age, what makes a Spiritual Covering so important in the Eye of God? In all simplicity, we have an intimate history from back then until now. Blasphemy, right? Wrong! Did we get here by ourselves? The answer is no. Our DNA is not a standalone one; we have a history, even if we know nothing about His Story. If we forget about the Promises of God, we cannot enforce them with the Blood of Jesus as a backup or as our Spiritual Atonement. Nor can we invoke the Holy Spirit as our Comforter as we should, especially when dealing with Divine Protection. Why? They are all CONNECTED...We are all CONNECTED. Once we disconnect, we lose our leverageable power.

Frankly, God wants us to use His Word as leverage with Him when contending or living life. So, if we remain silent, then things may not happen *As It Pleases God*. In layman's terms, we are left to our own devices. Here is what the scriptures want us to know: *"Out of heaven He let you hear His voice, that He might instruct you; on earth He showed you His great fire, and you heard His words out of the midst of the fire. And because He loved your fathers, therefore He chose their descendants after them; and He brought you out of Egypt with His Presence, with His mighty power, driving out from before you nations greater and mightier than you, to bring you in, to give you their land as an inheritance, as it is this day."* Deuteronomy 4:36-38.

How do we graft in our Spiritual Covering? We must know it is available to us. We must also place God first, knowing His Divine Location, redirecting all things on earth toward Heaven and vice versa. According to scripture, here is what it says: *"Therefore know this day, and consider it in your heart, that the LORD Himself is God in heaven above and on the earth beneath; there is no other."* Deuteronomy 4:39.

Secondly, Deuteronomy 4:39 says, "*You shall therefore keep His statutes and His commandments which I command you today, that it may go well with you and with your children after you, and that you may prolong your days in the land which the LORD your God is giving you for all time.*"

Thirdly, if one is ready for the Spiritual Transformation Process to take place, *As It Pleases God*, we must recite to our Heavenly Father: "*Every branch in Me that does not bear fruit take away; and every branch that bears fruit, prune that it may bear more fruit.*" John 15:2.

And fourthly, it is when God trusts us to complete our Divine Mission in the Spirit of Excellence amid hate, rejection, naysayers, or whatever is designed to beset us.

How do we know if we are on the right path? The first sign is when we can ABIDE in the Promises of God, *As It Pleases Him*, not ourselves. The second is when we become a FRIEND of God. Blasphemy, right? Wrong! According to scripture, "*You are My friends if you do whatever I command you. No longer do I call you servants, for a servant does not know what his master is doing; but I have called you friends, for all things that I heard from My Father I have made known to you.*" John 15:14-15. To be clear, before our Spiritual Status in the Kingdom is upgraded, we must become obedient servants first.

How do we know the difference between a servant and a friend status with God? For example, in the wee hours of the morning, when He calls our name, are we able to hear His Voice like the Prophet Samuel? Then again, when God sends specific instructions through an unconsuming burning bush as He did for Moses, are we able to hear His Voice? It is also noticed when God has placed Spiritual Tools in our hands to feed or deliver His sheep without fail. Although these are examples from the Bible, we all have the same potential. Yet, our untapped potential often goes unfounded, unused, underdeveloped, unrecognized, and so on.

However, on the other hand, disobedience will cause us to become an enemy of God, so tread carefully about what is laid at His Doorpost. Just remember this before any form of compromise: *"You did not choose Me, but I chose you and appointed you that you should go and bear fruit, and that your fruit should remain, that whatever you ask the Father in My name He may give you. These things I command you, that you love one another. If the world hates you, you know that it hated Me before it hated you. If you were of the world, the world would love its own. Yet because you are not of the world, but I chose you out of the world, therefore the world hates you. Remember the word that I said to you, 'A servant is not greater than his master.' If they persecuted Me, they will also persecute you. If they kept My word, they will keep yours also."* John 16-20. Taking a moment to reflect helps us keep our Spiritual Covering intact before our thoughts and emotions get the best of us.

Under the Veil

Engaging in the Promises of God and maintaining Spiritual Integrity does not necessitate perfection, an unrealistic standard. It requires AWARENESS! Once we recognize the lack of integrity in whatever or whomever, we can quickly repent, become a work-in-progress with a Divine Lesson or Principle in hand for the Kingdom, refine our skills, and push the boundaries to overcome our self-imposed limitations.

On the contrary, if we are NOT cognizant of our Spiritual Integrity, we can become easily blindsided, lose our Spiritual Covering, and have to play clean up after the fact. Meanwhile, this is what is happening under the veil, but not limited to such:

- ☐ We will lack self-control and NOT realize we are out of control while doing what it takes to get what we want, when we want it, how we want it, and with whom. And if someone gets in our way, we will remove them by any means necessary.

- ☐ We will lack growth, causing us to become stunted. As a result, we play pretend as if we have it going on, we put on a facade as if we know everything, or we use material gain or criticism to cover up our inadequacies or insecurities.

- ☐ We will engage in foolery while missing out on viable lessons. Whether it be through our words, actions, desires, biases, thoughts, or attitudes, we allow foolery and short-term pleasures to override our integral efforts while engaging in frivolous activities that do not contribute to our well-being or long-term growth.

- ☐ We will become paralyzed with the fear of failure, missing out on viable opportunities due to a bout with complacency, instead of embracing challenges and lessons to become better, stronger, proactive, and wiser.

- ☐ We will think everyone else has a problem while not being able to resolve our own issues. As a result, we will engage in behaviors that do not serve our best interests or the interests of those around us.

- ☐ We will seek the pleasures of life, not realizing we are yoked by the lust of the eyes, the lust of the flesh, and the pride of life.

Here is what we need to know about this matter: *"Likewise, exhort the young men to be sober-minded, in all things showing yourself to be a pattern of good works; in doctrine showing integrity, reverence,* incorruptibility, sound speech that cannot be condemned, that one who is an opponent may be ashamed, having nothing evil to say of you." Titus 2:6-8.

According to the Heavenly of Heavens, God wants us to become Spiritually Proactive, using the Word of God, the Fruits of the Spirit, and Christlike Character to change the trajectory of negativity and debauchery mid-air, imparting Divine Wisdom instead of profound foolery.

Using Pitch

With or without a *Spiritual Covering*, it is okay to work on ourselves on a moment-by-moment basis. Amid doing so, we must ask ourselves, 'What are we learning from this?' Then, document the answer, understand it according to scripture, and change our approach, *As It Pleases God*, without wallowing, complaining, fussing, fighting, or blaming. Does this work? Absolutely!

Experience is the best teacher as long as we learn, grow, and sow back into the Kingdom to build another, placing a Spiritual Seal on the Divine Wisdom gleaned. In my opinion, this is similar to how Noah sealed the Ark with pitch.

In all simplicity, seal your lessons with the Word of God to build your Alignment Prosthesis. Why is alignment artificial? The alignment is not artificial; the Spiritual Seal is the Artificial Branch that most will not have access to. "*And if some of the branches were broken off, and you, being a wild olive tree, were grafted in among them, and with them became a partaker of the root and fatness of the olive tree, do not boast against the branches. But if you do boast, remember that you do not support the root, but the root supports you.*" Romans 11:17-18.

This Artificial Branch helps us to exercise our Spiritual Discernment and connect to our Divine Helpers or VINES by allowing us to recognize them without rejecting them. For example, John 15:5 says, "*I am the vine, you are the branches. He who abides in Me, and I in him, bears much fruit; for without Me you can do nothing.*"

Spiritual Integrity

Most think that our personal integrity is the same as Spiritual Integrity, but they are like apples and oranges in the Eye of God. How so? Our personal integrity involves displaying, showing, or conducting ourselves a certain way in our professional, social, and personal interactions, which are sometimes limited to a specific group of people with all types of conditions, rules, and regulations having nothing to do with God Almighty. These ethics are often more prominent in our underlying idolatrous efforts and in excommunicating people who do not fit into our clique.

Meanwhile, *Spiritual Integrity* is about ALIGNING our Divine Values, Godly Standards, the Word of God, and the Fruits of the Spirit while behaving Christlike with HIGHER PRINCIPLES, such as compassion, honesty, love, mercy, and respect for all mankind. Should we not have limits? Absolutely. Matthew 7:6 says, "*Do not give what is holy to the dogs; nor cast your pearls before swine, lest they trample them under their feet, and turn and tear you in pieces.*"

Still, this does not give us the right to dog people out, mistreat, abuse, or degrade them. If we do, how then can we consider ourselves holy when we are behaving like them? How dare we consider ourselves holy when snubbing our noses at someone without offering a helping hand when it is within our power to do so!

Spiritual Integrity requires a connection to our moral compass (conscience, instincts, and discernment) and a *Spirit to Spirit* Connection to the Holy Trinity. More importantly, with Spiritual Integrity, God will also protect us amid the lies of another, especially if we are in Purpose on purpose. Therefore, we need only to worry about our Walk of Integrity, living by example, *As It Pleases Him*. What does this mean? Each man must account for his own.

For instance, imagine if you or someone else is engaging in deceitful behavior that causes harm. In such a situation, everyone needs to take responsibility, especially when the other person is acting with integrity.

Do we get a free pass in this situation, especially if we just had a moment or we made a mistake? I cannot determine who gets a free pass or not, but God will weigh the intents of the heart and the underlying trauma behind the lapse. However, I will say this: When operating WITHOUT deception or ill will, using the Fruits of the Spirit, Christlike Character, and the Word of God, He (the Holy Spirit) may step in to Divinely Assist, even if we fall short.

On the other hand, if we take ourselves to their level to correct them by acting or behaving like a fool with zero Spiritual Home Training, we are just as guilty, and God may or may not step up to assist. Plus, it may thrust us back into the Spiritual Classroom for remedial classes.

Personally, when dealing with the Promises of God, I would not want to take the risk of being led to the slaughter for taking things into my own hands, missing the Divine Mark due to the lack of self-control, having an emotional lapse, allowing my loose lips to sink my ship, or engaging in outright disobedience. Above all, to cultivate a sense of wholeness, *As It Pleases God*, we must exercise *Spiritual Integrity*, and we would definitely need to become *Spiritually Alert* to protect it.

Spiritually Alert

In the Promises of God, we must remain *Spiritually Alert* for real-time updates from the Heavenly of Heavens. How is this humanly possible? We must become fully present in the moment and pay attention to our thoughts, feelings, instincts, senses, dreams, synchronicities, intuitive nudges, and bodily sensations without judgment to develop a greater understanding of ourselves and how God speaks to us and through us.

More importantly, we must exhibit respect and gratefulness for them. If we do not, picturesquely, this is like opening the door for someone who did not say 'thank you' and spit in your face as they walked out the door. And then, the next time you saw them in that same store, you were Spiritually Alert and closed the door in their face to avoid being grossed out again by their spit. Of course, this was not out of revenge or spitefulness; you did not want them ruining your day with the stench of their spit in your face again. Nor did you want to become further traumatized by having to replay that moment in your head thousands of times over, repeating the same cycle. Well, our conscience, instincts, and nudges feel the same way! So, respect and thank them often, and they will serve you very, very well.

When it comes to remaining *Spiritually Alert*, this reminds me of the story of Abraham, Sarah, and Abimelech in Genesis 20. Here is part of the scripture, *"But God came to Abimelech in a dream by night, and said to him, indeed you are a dead man because of the woman whom you have taken, for she is a man's wife.' But Abimelech had not come near her; and he said, 'Lord, will You slay a righteous nation also? Did he not say to me, 'She is my sister?' And she, even she herself said, 'He is my brother.' In the integrity of my heart and innocence of my hands I have done this.' And God said to him in a dream, Yes, I know that you did this in the integrity of your heart. For I also withheld you from sinning against Me; therefore, I did not let you touch her. Now therefore, restore the man's wife; for he is a prophet, and he will pray for you and you shall live. But if you do not restore her, know that you shall surely die, you and all who are yours."* Genesis 20:3-7.

If Abimelech was not *Spiritually Alert*, he would NOT have heard or understood the Voice of God and would have heeded to his own demise. For this reason, we must develop the *Spirit to Spirit* Relationship to protect ourselves and our Bloodline against the lies of another, even if they are devout Believers.

Why is it important to Spiritually Protect ourselves, *As It Pleases God*? Regardless of who we are and why, we are all subject to err, especially when we are afraid, emotional, or traumatized. It is through God's Divine Grace and Mercy that we can repent on a moment-by-moment basis. In my opinion, it should not be taken for granted, misused, or use the crying wolf demeanor as a form of manipulation. Why should we not take this for granted? We need it available and on point when we REALLY need it the most!

Listen, to call forth a Legion of Angels at the drop of a dime is not something we should take for granted, and it is not just available to a few; it is available and PROMISED to all. We simply must know and understand how it works in the Kingdom of God while following the proper Spiritual Protocols set in place to avoid Spiritual Error on our behalf.

Then again, wasting time, fighting battles NOT of our own, and detouring our Divine Mission is something we need to outsource to the Source. What does outsourcing have to do with anything? It is always in our best interest to GRAFT IN the SOURCE to contend with anything or anyone having the potential to take us out of His Watchful Eye or out of Spiritual Covenant with Him. So, we must understand what it is:

- ☐ Heaven Sent.
- ☐ Self-sent.
- ☐ Self-induced.
- ☐ Self-created.
- ☐ Enemy-sent.

Regardless of where we are in life, God takes care of what belongs to Him. However, we should not take justice into our own hands; we must allow the Spirit of Justice from the Heavenly of Heavens to take over, keeping our hands clean in the Spirit of Excellence, using the Fruits of the Spirit, and behaving Christlike.

Here is a scripture to use with our prayers: *"LORD, You have heard the desire of the humble; You will prepare their heart; You will cause Your ear to hear, to do justice to the fatherless and the oppressed, that the man of the earth may oppress no more."* Psalm 10:17-18.

Opt for the Lesson

Even if we desire to seek payback, it is wise to cast it down and opt for the Spiritual Lesson instead. Why should we cast it down without seeking revenge? Unbeknown to most, the Divine Wisdom gleaned is far more VALUABLE than seeking revenge, nor do we want the zapping of the Spiritual Benefits associated. In my opinion, if we must endure, we may as well get something positive out of it, especially when it comes down to the Mysteries, Secrets, and Treasures of the Kingdom. So, let us align this accordingly: *"Good and upright is the LORD; therefore, He teaches sinners in the way. The humble He guides in justice, and the humble He teaches His way. All the paths of the LORD are mercy and truth, to such as keep His covenant and His testimonies."* Psalm 25:8-10.

According to the Heavenly of Heavens, to truly obtain the Promises of God, we must pride ourselves on treating people right, even if they have wronged us or refuse to admit to their debauchery. What if they take our kindness for a weakness? For the record, kindness is a hidden strength! In the Eye of God, it is only a weak individual who negates being kind. Really? Yes, really! It costs us NOTHING to be kind, but we can LOSE everything by NOT exhibiting kindness. So, please do not get this confused.

Spiritually Speaking, kindness goes a long way! Better yet, it goes much further than we think. It constitutes the saving and restoring of Bloodlines, Birthrights, and Blessings hidden or lost by another. If we desire to change the trajectory of our Legacies, we must take heed of how we treat others. Trust me, the Fruits of the Spirit and Christlike Character break Generational Curses. Without it, they become Spiritually Sealed, Compounded, and Transferred. What does this mean? Rotten fruits produce spoiled results continuously until someone wakes up from their slumber, doing what it takes to break the Spiritual Yoke, even if we appear to have it going on in the eyes of others.

Regardless of our perception of what we see around us, millions in the bank DO NOT equate to a million or billion-dollar positive mindset when it comes to the Promises of God. Blasphemy, right? Wrong! Let us try again with another question…A million-dollar or billion-dollar positive mindset means nothing if we are broke, right? Wrong again!

Divine Wisdom and Peace with Transferrable Growth and Provisions in or out of the Kingdom, *As It Pleases God*, is much desired for our Heaven on Earth Experience instead of a self-made or self-led squanderer. How is this possible when millions are millions, regardless of who possesses them? Point of fact, it is GREAT to have both, but it is improbable to have both without God, unless we are serving another god or worshiping a golden calf. *"Listen, my beloved brethren: Has God not chosen the poor of this world to be rich in faith and heirs of the kingdom which He promised to those who love Him? But you have dishonored the poor man. Do not the rich oppress you and drag you into the courts? Do they not blaspheme that noble name by which you are called? If you really fulfill the royal law according to the Scripture, 'You shall love your neighbor as yourself,' you do well; but if you show partiality, you commit sin, and are convicted by the law as transgressors."* James 2:5-9.

All in all, Spiritual Wealth and Physical Wealth are misunderstood by most. What is the difference? Simply put, Spiritual Wealth includes investments from the inside out with Divine Provisions according to our Divine Blueprint with no shame attached. Whereas, Physical Wealth is expendable capital from the outside with little or no Spiritual Investments from within. Nor does it align with the Kingdom or have God in the equation, but it does have hidden shame attached.

If we told the truth about our possessions or how we got to where we are today, would we get a side-eye from God or those around us? What is the purpose of knowing this information? *"The rich man's wealth is his strong city, and like a high wall in his own esteem."* Proverbs 18:11. In or out of the Kingdom, everything belongs to God! Tooting our own horns, especially when our inner city is in ruins due to our own making, causes us to create walls within the human psyche without realizing it until after the fact. How do I know? I have had views of it all: From the top looking down and from the bottom looking up...so when I swing the bat on this matter, I know what I am talking about!

Here is the deal: *"Wealth gained by dishonesty will be diminished, but he who gathers by labor will increase."* Proverbs 13:11. Frankly, honest or dishonest charactorial labor is how we know the difference between gaining righteously or unrighteously, and whether we are extending good or rotten fruits among the brethren. However, it should not stop us from changing the trajectory of our whatever with whomever. Nor should we fear Spiritual Wealth; we only need to tame our motives with outright humility, quickly forgiving ourselves and others.

What does humble forgiveness have to do with our Spiritual Power or Covering? First, all things are possible with God in Christ Jesus, especially if we let go of what and who keeps us bound Mentally, Physically, Emotionally, or Spiritually. Secondly, we never want to close the door on ourselves with kryptonic rotten fruits, corrupt character, or a bout with unforgiveness, causing us to lash out, traumatize, or abuse those who wholeheartedly have our back and those who do not.

In the Spirit of Truth and Transparency, God Blesses us to be a Blessing with the Hidden Power of Greatness, keeping the Well of Wealth overflowing in the Promises of God, *As It Pleases Him*. Once we engage in Kingdom Formality in such a manner with our Predestined Blueprint in hand, the Spiritual Covering Thermostat from the Heavenly of Heavens becomes set on AUTOMATIC.

CHAPTER 6
AUTHENTICITY

As God's authentic Masterpiece, we must also understand the Kingdom is around us and within us. Why must we become mindful of this fact? If we are divided against ourselves, we will fall to pieces quickly.

How can we avoid becoming divided, *As It Pleases God*? We must become excellent problem-solvers or problem-resolvers. Are they not the same? According to the Heavenly of Heavens, a problem-solver has a definite solution that we must find. In contrast, a problem-resolver creates a solution to facilitate a win-win, even when the odds are against them.

Anyone can become a problem-solver with a little training or adaptation. In taking this a step further, we must become a little more CREATIVE to become or evolve into an effective problem-resolver in or out of the Kingdom, *As It Pleases God*. What does this mean in layman's terms? In the Eye of God, solving problems as it pleases us is not going to get it. We must become Divinely Creative at working on ourselves, fixing our issues first, and then becoming an example for others through the POWER hidden in our Testimony with a RESOLVE. Talk is cheap; we can say anything and believe it to be true, yet still a lie. However, taking action, *As It Pleases God*, changes the trajectory of whatever, with whomever, with a work-in-progress mentality.

Plus, any form of Kingdom Impact requires us to think inside, outside, around, through, over, and under the box, leaving no stone unturned. Why should we leave no stone unturned in the Eye of God? All the information we need is already. We only need to align ourselves to receive it, *As It Pleases God*.

Now, to create a Spiritual Seal for the *Spirit to Spirit* transfer of information, we must give THANKS for the information in advance. Let me back up for a moment…It is Actionable Thanks, to be exact, and it will gracefully yield on our behalf, especially if our worthiness or trustworthiness is established.

How can we possibly establish ourselves to receive or transfer information with our actionable efforts, *As It Pleases God*? Listed below are a few ways, but not limited to such:

- ☐ Document precisely what the mission, goal, problem, or intent is while understanding what it is not.

- ☐ Ask the right fact-finding questions in the *What, When, Where, How, Why,* and with *Whom* forms to absolve the guesswork with absolutes.

- ☐ Develop a system or strategy surrounding our answers, putting quality over quantity to establish value.

- ☐ Mind Map the Plan of Action to establish resilience by having a check and balance system, painting a visible and mental picture with the least amount of effort. Remember, SIMPLICITY is key; COMPLEXITY is a problem.

- ☐ Document the points of execution with a step-by-step process while continuing to learn and improve daily. With the placates of *Authenticity*, we must break the giant steps down into small ones, allowing us to fill in the gaps easily.

- [ ] We must list the benefits, win-wins, relatabilities, or takeaways of the cooperative efforts. It helps us figure out the unfigurable, making them configurable in the Eye of God and sparking our Creative Genius.

- [ ] Document the obstacles or cause-and-effect to proactively counteract or error-proof them in advance.

- [ ] Allocate how much time will be spent, or allot a specific time of day to strategize, meditate, think, or brainstorm with others.

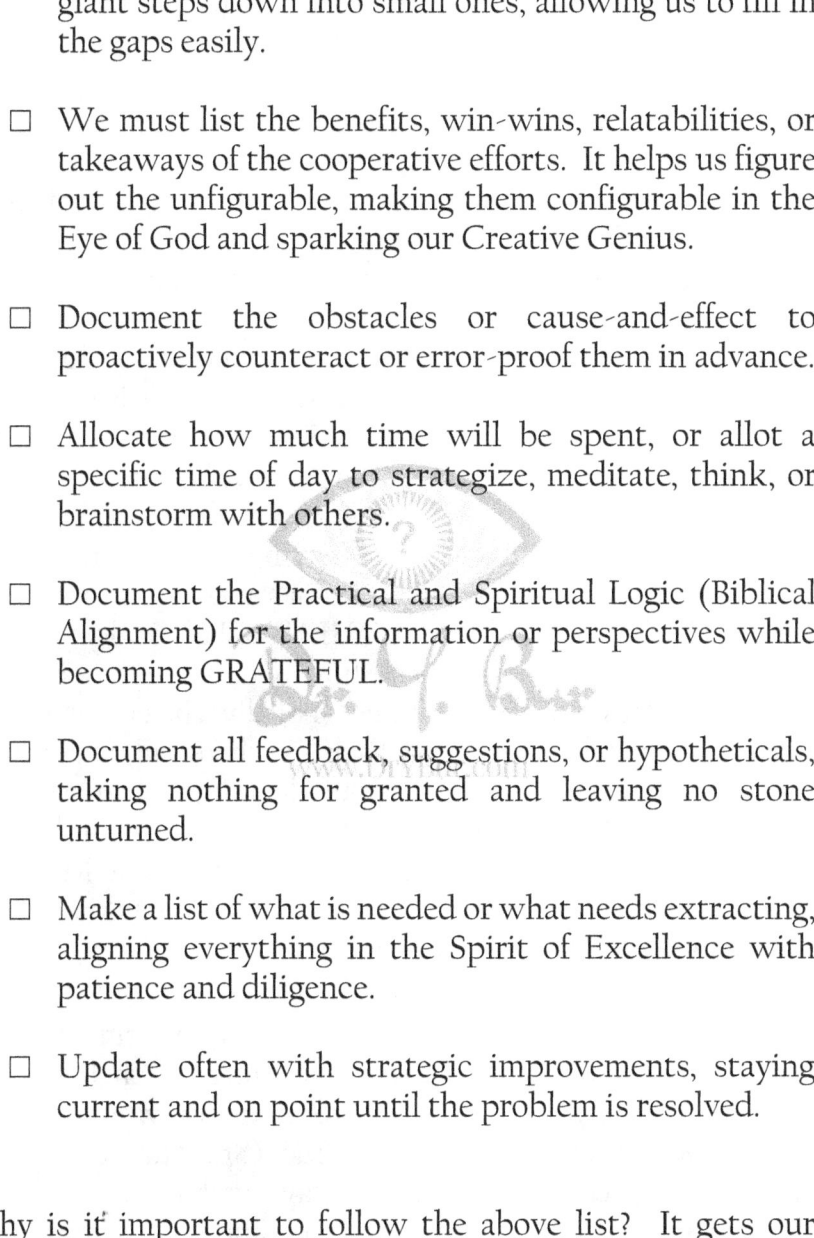

- [ ] Document the Practical and Spiritual Logic (Biblical Alignment) for the information or perspectives while becoming GRATEFUL.

- [ ] Document all feedback, suggestions, or hypotheticals, taking nothing for granted and leaving no stone unturned.

- [ ] Make a list of what is needed or what needs extracting, aligning everything in the Spirit of Excellence with patience and diligence.

- [ ] Update often with strategic improvements, staying current and on point until the problem is resolved.

Why is it important to follow the above list? It gets our wheels turning in the right direction, *As It Pleases God*. Plus, when we master the ability to document in our own words without plagiarizing, we will be better at querying ourselves,

God, the Holy Spirit, people, and life. More importantly, it helps us to think on our feet, primarily when the enemy aims to sweep us off them.

How is it possible not to plagiarize, especially when we have to learn from someone, something, or someplace? The mindset God desires from us is to MASTER the ability to write a book report or summarize from our personal perspective about what we are gleaning, instead of becoming a parroting cat.

As a Word to the Wise, there should be a difference between what I said, what you heard, and what is conveyed. Why should there be a difference? First, when the Holy Spirit is involved, Divine Wisdom is ENCODED, taking Him to DECODE for others. Secondly, we are different, speaking different Spiritual Languages and having varying Blueprints.

Unfortunately, based on my Predestined Blueprint, if my tongue becomes another, AUTHENTICITY is lost in the Spiritual Transfer, and this is how we 'get got' when the enemy challenges or provokes us. Thirdly, the enemy knows when we are faking it better than us; therefore, it creates a bullseye of weakness when it should be our greatest strength.

Listen, God will speak our language to us, and when dealing with our Predestined Blueprint, we must MASTER the ability to hear correctly to Spiritually Download at the drop of a dime. For this reason, journaling or note-taking is extremely important in our *Spirit to Spirit* Conversations with our Heavenly Father to develop *Authenticity* in bringing forth our Divine Blueprint. More importantly, it helps us to EXTRACT the information, instructions, or whatever, and CONVERT it into our own tongue (Spiritual Language). Really? Yes, really! In the same way, we have our TYPE of whatever; we also have a LANGUAGE, and if we do not know what it is, it is time to get in the know. If not, what we do not know will get us.

When dealing with the right or wrong cat, our summarized perspectives will help us hone in on our uniqueness, causing us to want to be ourselves and overcome the copycat syndrome easily besetting us in the Eye of God. In addition, our summarized perspectives, *As It Pleases Him*, will help us to dissect and process information based on how it applies to us, our Spiritual Journey, or our Divine Blueprint.

Divine Triggering

According to the Heavenly of Heavens, God allows people to inspire, mentor, confirm, or trigger Divine Greatness from within, aligning with our Predestined Blueprint or Spiritual Classroom.

Once again, we are all different, with lessons that must be learned or preparational processes that must occur. If we do not know how we are different or what we must learn in the Eye of God, then why are we covering it up, diluting it, or polluting it with worldly information instead of Divine Revelation, *As It Pleases Him*?

In reality, we would never expect a professional athlete not to train, but based on their phenomenal skills and training for our entertainment, they get paid very well. So, why are we walking around Spiritually Untrained in Kingdom Principles, Laws, and Protocols?

Do we think the Benefits of the Kingdom are not profitable? Maybe or maybe not, but when one needs what money, fame, or fortune cannot buy, we will heed the CALL of *Authenticity*. How do I know? The Spiritual Notches on my belt came at a HIGH PRICE with a lot of training, preparation, and chastisement, and I would never wish it upon anyone. Hence, with my Authentic Self, I give freely to thee. All we need is an OPPORTUNITY to understand from God's Divine Perspective, which will change our Spiritual Trajectories from pleasing ourselves to *As It Pleases Him*.

It Is For You

Here is the deal: *How To Please God* is not for me, but for you! The opportune information is on the Spiritual Table; you can take it or leave it. Is this not a little insensitive? Maybe or maybe not; yet, when the Bridegroom comes, you need to be ready and adequately adorned with the Spiritual Fruits and Christlike Character for the Spiritual Seal. If not, your sensitivities will not save you, nor will they wait for you to get it together.

Nevertheless, when Spiritually Gleaning from the Divine Reservoir of Wisdom or Revelational Knowledge, we DO NOT want to become a copycat victim, predator, or parroting cat. What is the purpose of exercising caution in this area? We cannot distinguish who is speaking and who is not. Unfortunately, this inadvertently causes us to become entangled in Spiritual Mesh with a form of godliness but NOT Godly, triggering our Spiritual Lamps to burn out prematurely or run out of oil quickly.

When operating with zero Spiritual Fruits or without Christlike Character, it is only a matter of time before we 'get got' with false measures. What do false measures have to do with the transfer of information? By not developing our own VOICE, *As It Pleases God*, we allow our weaknesses, biases, conditioning, and traumas to speak or absorb like a sponge without our Spiritual Discerning Faculties kicking in.

False Measures

What is the purpose of exhibiting caution with *False Measures* or worldliness? *False Measures* ruin our *Authenticity*, hindering us from coming into our own and blocking our Spiritual Gifts and Purpose!

Not knowing our Predestined Blueprint, *As It Pleases God*, blocks our Inner Genius, preventing us from working on ourselves as we should. As a result, it replaces it with insecurities, causing us to jump from one thing to the next, looking for fame, fortune, status, recognition, or a quick fix. Unbeknown to most, the inferiority complex keeps the human psyche yoked by negative characteristics such as jealousy, envy, pride, greed, coveting, and competitiveness, leading to all sorts of underlying idolatry or undesirable plagues.

How do we know if we are consumed with a Copycat Spirit under false measures? First and foremost, we know when we are not being our true selves. We do not need anyone to confirm we are negatively consumed...the conscience already knows, even if we pretend to be unaware of it. Secondly, it is often noticed in the lack of consistency, dullness, lukewarmness, and the lies we tell ourselves and others. Thirdly, it is known in the quality of our fruits, even if we attempt to justify, downplay, or up-play them. And fourthly, we do not know our WHEN. When we do not master how to change the language at the drop of a dime, we will find ourselves speaking out of turn, over-talking someone to be heard, showing off how much we know, speaking over someone's head, talking down to others, and so on.

What is the big deal, especially when we know what we know? Regardless of how much we know or do not know, speaking out of season can create undue cycles of remedial efforts. For example, we are excellent at work but suck at being good husbands, fathers, mothers, or wives. We are excellent at being fathers or mothers, but cannot keep a job to feed or provide for our family. We are great at attracting a mate but cannot keep one, as we go from relationship to relationship, thinking everyone else has the problem. Then again, it can prevent the Holy Spirit from speaking Divine Wisdom on our behalf.

Are we not all entitled to receive the Knowledge or Wisdom of God? Of course, we are entitled, but it does not give us the Divine Keys to the Kingdom of Heaven. We must put in the work to Spiritually Till our own ground regarding our seeds, fruits, and seasons. Why must we work on our seeds and fruits? When we lack the humility needed to become Spiritually Awakened or develop a *Spirit to Spirit* Relationship, we misuse it for selfish gain or a power play. Therefore, we must be Spiritually Trained to deal with, understand, or relate to all things SPIRITUAL to gain the *Keys to the Kingdom*.

Keys to the Kingdom

Everyone wants the *Keys to the Kingdom*, but most of us do not want to put in the work that is required of us, even though the desire for success and achievement is at an all-time high, breaking all types of records. Still, in the Eye of God, we are missing the mark. Why? We are getting the keys to the wrong kingdom with overnight success and instant gratification, omitting the factors of putting in the hard work and Spiritually Tilling our own grounds.

Although we have free will to choose the origination and destination of our keys, we have gotten into the habit of blaming God, our Heavenly Father, when things do not work out as planned. Now, the question on the table is, 'Why should He take the blame for something we did not include Him in?' Then again, 'Why would we put in all the hard work, dedication, and perseverance without Him?' Is it because we know that it is a 'No Go' with Him involved? Or is it that we are taking shortcuts, quick fixes, or the easy way out, hoping to bypass the hard work? Clearly, there is no pun intended with these questions; I am only here to get your mental wheels turning in the correct direction.

What are the *Keys to the Kingdom*? Our Spiritual Keys could be or mean a lot of things. Here are some Spiritual Keys that will serve us very well, but not limited to such:

- ☐ We have the Key of Respect.
- ☐ We have the Key to the Fruits of the Spirit. (Love, Joy, Peace, Patience, Kindness, Goodness, Faithfulness, Gentleness, and Self-Control).
- ☐ We have the Key of Hope.
- ☐ We have the Key of Repentance.
- ☐ We have the Key of Prayer.
- ☐ We have the Key of Fasting.
- ☐ We have the Keys of Wisdom, Knowledge, Power, and Understanding.
- ☐ We have the Key of Forgiveness.
- ☐ We have the Key of Compassion.
- ☐ We have the Key of Mercy.
- ☐ We have the Key of Sharing.
- ☐ We have the Key of Obedience.

God does not expect us to become perfect with the *Keys to the Kingdom* overnight; however, He requires us to work on them consistently. If we focus on one key a month, by the end of the year, we will find that our life will take on a whole new form, gaining more access to our Spiritual Significance, GUARANTEED.

Spiritual Reshuffling

What is more, if we are caught up in too many distractions leading us away from our Purpose, we will find that we will begin to live our lives through the lenses of another. When we become addicted to the opinions of others while living a life of show and pretense, *Divine Authenticity* gets lost in the shuffle. Then again, it may lead to God RESHUFFLING the deck occasionally, waking us up from our Spiritual Slumber.

If a *Spiritual Reshuffling* happens, DO NOT become alarmed; it happens to us all. We all can become easily sidetracked, brainwashed, or provoked in the areas where we are weak, have developed a sore spot, or have experienced some form of trauma. The key is NOT to panic; get back on track, learn, understand, revamp if necessary, document, share, and keep it moving. Besides, it keeps our *Authenticity* potent in the Eye of God.

How does a *Spiritual Reshuffling* make us potent? Our GREATNESS depends on us pulling through, enabling us to shine brightly from the inside out with a Heavenly Glow to share our experiences of wisdom.

What is the purpose of sharing after a *Spiritual Reshuffling*? The Experience of Wisdom teaches us what a textbook cannot, making us EFFECTIVE at doing what we do. However, we cannot ignore our relevance when dealing with *Authenticity* in the Eye of God. We must learn to ask the right questions in our *Spirit to Spirit* alone time and be ready to document to keep the Heavenly Flow active, *As It Pleases God*.

In Sparking the Heavenly Flow of Divine Wisdom, it is imperative to pinpoint the applicable scriptures to establish Divine Leverage amid the *Spiritual Reshuffling* process. Once done, listed below are a few questions to ask or answer in our *Spirit to Spirit* Conversations, but not limited to such:

The questions to ask God are:

- ☐ What do I need to learn?
- ☐ What is the lesson?
- ☐ Where did I go wrong?
- ☐ How did I get off track?
- ☐ Can You show me the purpose of this ordeal?
- ☐ What did I miss?
- ☐ How can I help others with this experience?
- ☐ What is the WISDOM I need to extract or convert?

- ☐ What is the plan?
- ☐ Can You show me the way?
- ☐ Lord, can You take the wheel?
- ☐ Father, can You show me the win-win?

The questions to answer for yourself are:

- ☐ How would you feel if that happened to you?
- ☐ What was the meaning or objective behind that?
- ☐ How did it make you feel?
- ☐ What did you gain?
- ☐ What would be a better approach?
- ☐ Do you think that was the best way of handling it?
- ☐ What provoked you in such a manner?
- ☐ What were you feeling or thinking about when it happened?
- ☐ How can you create a win-win?
- ☐ Where is the love in that?
- ☐ Did you listen before jumping the gun on your response?
- ☐ Would God frown upon the way you handled this?

When *Authentically* approaching God, *Spirit to Spirit*, we will learn the value of the REVERSAL process, *As It Pleases Him*. We can develop our own list of questions or responses to provoke the element of thought without offending, grieving, or blaspheming the Holy Spirit. Once we learn the power encapsulated in asking the right questions, we position ourselves to embrace our Authentic Achievement process or Divine Mastery without second-guessing ourselves.

Always remember, it is NOT what we say; it is HOW we say it. So, if we develop a soft approach with love, kindness, compassion, and a soft tone of voice, we can accomplish more

Mentally, Physically, Emotionally, and Spiritually. More importantly, by including Him in our equational efforts, we can better flip the script on our story, our life, or the narrative on anything to create a win-win without becoming manipulative.

How can we reverse anything without becoming somewhat manipulative? When dealing with God, *Spirit to Spirit*, there is no Spiritual Law against quoting APPLICABLE scriptures back to Him regarding a situation, circumstance, or event. Spiritually Speaking, He prefers us to know what we are talking about and do our homework instead of coming to His Divine Throne, empty-handed, babbling, complaining, begging, selfishly siccing Him on people, or attempting to prostitute Him as if He can be bought, sold, manipulated, or bartered at will.

In addition, in the *Spiritual Reshuffling* process, there is no Spiritual Law against using the Fruits of the Spirit to reverse any negative fruits into positive ones to become Christlike. Plus, there is No Spiritual Law preventing us from wanting to become better, stronger, and wiser, *As It Pleases Him*, according to our Blueprinted Purpose. With all else, we must know the Spiritual Laws, Principles, and Protocols when engaging. Hence, it behooves us to become *Spiritually Interdependent* and stand at attention with the Holy Trinity at full alert 24/7 and *Be You*.

Being You

Are you content with *Being You*? Are you afraid of being who you are? Do you wish you were someone else? Do you not know that God is within you?

As It Pleases God, He needs more from within us than what is residing outside of us. How is this possible when He is invisible? His invisibility does not mean that He is not present! Nor does it mean that He made a mistake when He created you. God needs your gratefulness and for you to *Be You*.

Why is gratefulness so important when being our authentic selves? The Kingdom is within you, and the moment you are ungrateful for *Being You*, it is reflected in the Kingdom of God. Blasphemy, right? Wrong. Please allow me to Spiritually Align: "*So Jesus answered and said, 'Were there not ten cleansed? But where are the nine? Were there not any found who returned to give glory to God except this foreigner?' And He said to him, 'Arise, go your way. Your faith has made you well.' Now when He was asked by the Pharisees when the Kingdom of God would come, He answered them and said, The Kingdom of God does not come with observation; nor will they say, 'See here!' or 'See there!' For indeed, the Kingdom of God is within you.*" Luke 17:17-21. Do not be fooled by foolery; instead, look within to extract the GRATEFULNESS designed to heal you from the inside out and establish value.

Why must we value ourselves? First, it cuts down on the Spiritual Violations easily besetting us. Secondly, it eliminates bogus requests such as praying for bigger lips when He gave us a mouth to speak, praying for a pair of shoes when He gave us feet to walk, or praying for someone's breath when He gave us the ability to kindly hand them a breath mint without talking about them behind their back.

Most of our Spiritual Issues surround the lack of *Authenticity* and wanting what does not belong to us, even if we pretend that this is not true. Yet, the Spiritual Statistics from the Heavenly of Heavens do not lie; we are dividing ourselves without realizing it. Then again, we may know it, but we do not care because we have not yet developed value in ourselves. Is this really happening? Absolutely.

Everyone wants to be someone or something they are not without finetuning who they are from the inside out, perfecting and working with what they have, or giving attention to their Predestined Blueprint. Well, maybe not everyone, but 99.9% of us are guilty of this, and I am not excluded from this statistic. Really? Yes, really! It is in our DNA. For this reason, we must Spiritually Till our own ground, which means that we must do this for ourselves.

Listen, we can buy into the new normal if we like, but if we look at the mental health statistics, they are on the rise, more so than ever before in the history of mankind. Why is this happening to us? Suppose we keep lying to ourselves about who we are or refuse to incorporate Godly Character into our daily lifestyle. In this case, we become susceptible to the intricacies associated with low self-esteem appearing high.

If we dare to take a trip down memory lane to our childhood upbringing, we were not born online. We must learn how to rightly divide our online world from reality. If not, we can lose our identity by desiring to become someone else or coveting them without knowing them.

Now, take a moment to look around; how many people look the same? No one, right? Even identical twins appear similar but very different in their own unique way in the Eye of God. We must cut the superficial illusion of being a specific size, color, build, shape, status, or having specific features to gauge our *Spiritual Authenticity* or Worthiness. Please allow me to Spiritually Align before going deeper, *"Do not look at his appearance or at his physical stature, because I have refused him. For the LORD does not see as man sees; for man looks at the outward appearance, but the LORD looks at the heart."* 1 Samuel 16:7.

In the Eye of God, we are out of order if we spend more time on our outer adornment than on our inner adornment. From a Spiritual Perspective, the ultimate goal is to become and remain healthy, Mentally, Physically, Emotionally, and Spiritually. By working on our *Authentic Selves* from the inside out, there is no limit on what we can achieve, *As It Pleases Him.*

In preparing ourselves, *As It Pleases God*, we must understand that everything we need is already. What are we preparing for that is already? We prepare for the Divine

Opportunities of the Kingdom or our Predestined Blueprint by eliminating the excess negative baggage, negative thoughts, destructive behaviors, stiff-necked tendencies, and rough edges. Does this really make a difference? Of course, it does. After Jesus chose His disciples, He trained them in the IMAGE of what was already within them.

In developing our *Authenticity*, we must get out of our own way. Now, since we are all different, there is no 100% foolproof or cookie-cutter way. Nevertheless, we must get out of the mindset of thinking that something is wrong with us. Then focus on what is RIGHT, becoming a work-in-progress, *As It Pleases God*. What makes this so important in the Eye of God? There is good in everyone, and it is our responsibility to locate it and capitalize on it.

What are the indications of standing in our own way? It will vary from person to person, situation to situation, trauma to trauma, and so on. Nevertheless, listed below are a few obstructive indicators, but not limited to such:

- ☐ We obstruct ourselves when making excuses.
- ☐ We obstruct ourselves when blaming others.
- ☐ We obstruct ourselves when making assumptions.
- ☐ We obstruct ourselves when shifting responsibility.
- ☐ We obstruct ourselves when worrying a lot.
- ☐ We obstruct ourselves when we procrastinate.
- ☐ We obstruct ourselves when we are critical.
- ☐ We obstruct ourselves when we are very chaotic.
- ☐ We obstruct ourselves when we are addicted to drama.
- ☐ We obstruct ourselves when we are abusive.
- ☐ We obstruct ourselves when we lack tongue control.
- ☐ We obstruct ourselves when our attitudes suck.
- ☐ We obstruct ourselves with uncontrollable anger.
- ☐ We obstruct ourselves when we are manipulative.
- ☐ We obstruct ourselves when we are compulsive liars.
- ☐ We obstruct ourselves when we do not listen.

- ☐ We obstruct ourselves when we are rebellious.
- ☐ We obstruct ourselves when we are negative.
- ☐ We obstruct ourselves when we are easily provoked.
- ☐ We obstruct ourselves when we lack self-control.

These indicators are not set in stone but can hinder us immensely, especially in seeking *Authenticity* according to our Predestined Blueprint and *As It Pleases God*. Remember, what worked in one phase of our lives may not work in the next. Amid all:

- ☐ We must understand our possibilities.
- ☐ We must understand our limitations.
- ☐ We must understand our expectations.
- ☐ We must understand our mannerisms.
- ☐ We must understand whether we are leaders, followers, influencers, or agitators.

What is the purpose of knowing this? Sometimes, we leave little room for error, so we must remove false expectations. Doing so allows us to become students to temporarily bring forth certain Divine Information, Principles, and Wisdom. Then again, we may have to instigate an inner reckoning to bring forth the Diamond in the Rough through *Spiritual Interdependence*. Who knows, right? Nevertheless, when *Pleasing God*, the ultimate goal is to become *Authentically You*, doing what you were created to do.

CHAPTER 7
SPIRITUAL INTERDEPENDENCE

God is not expecting perfection; He expects obedience as we operate in the Spirit of Excellence. Why does He expect Spiritual Excellence? When dealing with our Gifts, Calling, Talents, and Creativity, we all have something we are good at to *'Give Back'* to the Kingdom of Heaven as a token of appreciation.

Is perfection and the Spirit of Excellence the same? No, they are not. In the Kingdom, perfection is faultless, needing no correction. In contrast, the Spirit of Excellence does what it takes to get it right, build quality, develop durability, or create a win-win.

In the world we live in today, we spend a lot of time responding or reacting, omitting the benefits encapsulated in corresponding, relating, and listening. When we are proactively on the defense, getting information in or out of us without ulterior motives becomes difficult, making us secretly resistant to change. How is this possible when we are trustworthy team players? All we need to do is check our thoughts and level of discipline.

We are fine if our chatter or discipline is positive, productive, and fruitful. If our internal dialogue is negative, unproductive, unfruitful, and we are trying to take over or control everything, we have work to do. In essence, if we do not get to the root or face our truths, regrafting from negative to positive, it will affect our outcomes or put a dent in our Kingdom Impact when we least expect it.

More importantly, we must dust ourselves off when we fall short and begin again. Every day is filled with new opportunities, bridging our failures together for the ultimate showdown of success. It is not wise to allow yesterday's problems to become an issue the next day. In the Eye of God, they are simply lessons, experiences, wisdom, information, and tools; all we need to do is avail ourselves to this form of Spiritual Classroom, *As It Pleases Him.*

How can a Spiritual Classroom benefit us when the Spirit of the Lord comes upon us? We are all different without a cookie-cutter way of Spiritual Approach or Reproach; therefore, it will vary from person to person, circumstance to circumstance, region to region, condition to condition, trauma to trauma, and so on.

Why are our Spiritual Classrooms or Lessons not set in stone? Regarding the Kingdom, we are not robots or overnight sensations. We must be trained, equipped, tested, and commissioned based on our abilities and Divine Blueprint. Simply put, what works for one person may not necessarily work for another.

For example, my Spiritual Training would wipe out those not born with specific Spiritual Tools or Anointings. For this reason, we should NOT play around with Spiritual Things we do not understand. Why? We can unawaringly open the door to the enemy without realizing it. Nonetheless, getting back to my example, SEEING or HEARING as I do, would shake the average person to the core, making them Kingdomly Unusable in the Eye of God. Meanwhile, being that I am Divinely Commission to do what I do for my Heaven on Earth Experience, and according to my Predestined Blueprint, with Spiritual Principles in hand, I do not flinch an inch.

What is the purpose of not flinching? Flinching with our mouths wide open or having our feelings on our shoulders lets the enemy know where our heads are. Then again, it can clue them in on where our weaknesses are.

Standing our ground in the Realm of the Spirit takes discipline and good character. Why must we stand our ground? The enemy will not tempt us with people, places, and things we DO NOT like or will not provoke us. He is coming with our TYPE, period. Now, if we do not know what our type is or is not, our worthiness can become contaminated, creating doubt and instability within the human psyche.

What if we are Believers, and the enemy cannot touch us? Unfortunately, this is how we 'get got' publicly and privately. The enemy does not need to touch, mishandle, or get in our faces as most think. The SEEDS are planted Mentally, Physically, and Emotionally, invoking shame, insecurities, abandonment, or triggers. What makes this so important as Believers? They cause us to turn on ourselves with negativity, debauchery, and waywardness associated with the lust of the eyes, the lust of the flesh, and the pride of life. For this reason, we cannot point the finger at what appears as the enemy; we need to check our character, fruits, motives, inner chatter, and mindset FIRST.

Self-Analysis

Why must we do a *Self-Analysis* before pointing the finger? If we behave and think like the enemy, then they do not need to do anything. We self-destruct on our own while missing the mark or move of God. Really? Yes, really! We cannot proclaim Divine Holiness while acting, behaving, thinking waywardly, or treating God's precious sheep like junkyard dogs, traumatizing them because they appear less than us, or we think we know more than them. Yet, in Earthen Vessels, we walk around calling evil good and good evil, not knowing the difference between Spiritual Duality, as the enemy sits back, laughing at us.

Then, as the enemy gets a kick out of our Spiritual Oversights, we sit back, making excuses as if God wants someone to suffer to avoid our secretly selfish atrocities from becoming our public shame. Is this really happening? Absolutely! My question is, 'Who is winning here?' Is the enemy winning? Are our hidden secrets winning? Or is it our secret fears? Regardless of who wins, the Kingdom of God will Divinely Unveil itself with or without us; therefore, it behooves us to jump on board because the fight is FIXED.

What if it is not our fight? We are ONE in the Kingdom. Although no one is perfect, everyone must do their part or try their best to right their wrongs, *As It Pleases God*. Regardless of our feelings or thoughts, we must prepare ourselves, fruits, character, seeds, and BLOODLINE to deal with or handle God's Divine Move.

If we have not developed a *Spirit to Spirit* Relationship with the Holy Trinity, it is best to get the ball rolling before the shaking occurs. Please allow me to align accordingly: "*Now this, 'Yet once more,' indicates the removal of those things that are being shaken, as of things that are made, that the things which cannot be shaken may remain. Therefore, since we are receiving a kingdom which cannot be shaken, let us have grace, by which we may serve God acceptably with reverence and godly fear.*" Hebrews 12:27-28.

Would You Know?

In the Kingdom's Fixed Fight, establishing *Spiritual Interdependence* costs us nothing to be KIND to all; therefore, "*Do not forget to entertain strangers, for by so doing some have unwittingly entertained angels.*" Hebrews 13:2. What makes this so important in the Eye of God? Believer or not, the way God trains, molds, tests, or empowers us with lessons, information, or whatever may not appear as we think. But the question is, 'Would you know when they appear?'

Here is what we must know before going any further: "*To the general assembly and church of the firstborn who are registered in heaven, to God the Judge of all, to the spirits of just men made perfect, to Jesus the Mediator of the new covenant, and to the blood of sprinkling that speaks better things than that of Abel. See that you do not refuse Him who speaks. For if they did not escape who refused Him who spoke on earth, much more shall we not escape if we turn away from Him who speaks from heaven, whose voice then shook the earth; but now He has promised, saying, 'Yet once more I shake not only the earth, but also heaven.'*" Hebrews 12:23-26.

Amid this Divine Movement of God, I cannot mention how often I have been overlooked or kicked to the curb. It only caused me to shake my head in utter dismay with an understanding beyond human reasoning. What would cause an oversight as such? I did not appear as the Messenger, a Well of Divine Wisdom, or to have the ANSWER to their questions or petitions.

To add insult to injury, they proclaimed to be Holy Ghost-Filled and Fire-Baptized. So, in this proclamation process, I receive my message, and you mean to tell me the Holy Spirit did not clue them in on who He sent? Come on…we have to do better than this. What is the big deal, especially when we are all subjected to error? Spirit knows Spirit!

More importantly, if the Holy Spirit did not give them a heads-up, neither will I! I keep it moving in the Spirit of Excellence, bearing no grudges. Why? I will glean the information or lesson to feed God's sheep, period! Then, move to the next Spiritual Assignment without wasting time. Besides, if the enemy recognizes me, shooting their shots, one would think my own would recognize me, right? Frankly, if they recognized me, I would not have the information to validate my Spiritual Seal or put the enemy to boot.

According to the Heavenly of Heavens, we damage ourselves, our seeds, and our fruits by NOT incorporating God into our equational efforts or becoming a work-in-progress, *As*

It Pleases Him. More importantly, we will become selfish by default when omitting the Blood of Jesus as a Spiritual Covering and the Holy Spirit as our Spiritual Guide.

As Trustworthy Team Players, *As It Pleases God*, we must use the Holy Spirit to GUIDE us and the Blood of Jesus to COVER us. What can this do for us? Listed below are a few profound BENEFITS to embrace, but not limited to such:

- ☐ We will experience placement growth and become fruitful from the inside out.

- ☐ We will experience a peaceful rest beyond human understanding.

- ☐ We will have access to Supernatural Wisdom, gaining access to the Secrets, Mysteries, and Principles of the Kingdom to create a Divine Flow.

- ☐ We will have Divine Understanding, keeping us '*In The Spiritual Know.*'

- ☐ We will have the Spirit of Counsel, guiding and advising on all things Spiritual and earthly.

- ☐ We will have the Spirit of Knowledge that is teaching, training, and strengthening us on a moment-by-moment basis.

- ☐ We will have a fearful reverence of God, keeping us humble, respectful, repenting, and prayerful.

Here is the scripture to align the *Spiritual Interdependence* benefits: "*There shall come forth a Rod from the stem of Jesse, and a Branch shall grow out of his roots. The Spirit of the LORD shall rest upon*

Him, the Spirit of Wisdom and Understanding, the Spirit of Counsel and Might, The Spirit of knowledge and of the fear of the LORD." Isaiah 11:1-2. What is the purpose of these benefits? They will help to avoid bringing shame to our names and the Kingdom while polishing our Fruits of the Spirit and Christlike Character to create excellent *People Skills*.

Enough is Enough

The Sanctuary or Temple of God is within, and most often, this is where we stop. What causes the Spiritual Halt? We say we are the Sanctuary or Temple, yet we fail to safeguard the Mind, Body, Soul, and Spirit with the proper Spiritual Adornment, *As It Pleases God*. As a result, we find ourselves becoming people-pleasers outwardly, attempting to fill the hidden void from within.

What do we need to do to fill the void? We need to get the specific details on what God expects from each of us, which requires that we engage in a *Spirit to Spirit* Relationship for Divine Instructions. For the record, we do not have any Authentic Prophets in the Bible who did not seek SPECIFIC INSTRUCTIONS from God. Yet, in today's time, we operate as if Divine Instructions are prepackaged on a shelf for sale. To add insult to injury, amid the sale of the information, they know it is lacking the Spiritual Anointing from the Heavenly of Heavens, but attempt to stamp God's Divine Approval anyway. The moment we attempt to sell the instructions commercially while lying on Him, we become at odds with God, zapping our authentic peace and joy, causing us to play pretend.

Why would the Spirit of Pretense consume us, especially when we are delivering the Word of God? Everyone is different with a unique Blueprint; therefore, we must know the difference between Divine Provisions and Greed when attempting to prepackage God, place Him in a box without a *Spirit to Spirit* Connection, to simply capitalize on the vulnerabilities of His sheep, or cut corners to pad our pockets! And God is saying to us, *Enough is Enough!*

All in all, when we are properly aligned in a *Spirit to Spirit* Relationship, God will get the Divine Information or Instructions to us by any means necessary; we only need to TAP IN, *As It Pleases Him!* What is the purpose of doing so? Point in fact, "*Surely the Lord GOD does nothing, unless He reveals His SECRET to His Servants the Prophets.*" Amos 3:7. In all simplicity, if you are on Divine Assignment for Him, the Divine Information will flow to you. No lies necessary...All He needs from you is the WILLINGNESS to embrace *Spiritual Interdependence*, and He will work out the kinks.

Spiritual Interdependence is the way to go when dealing with the enemy's wiles. However, avoiding the attacks, distractions, temptations, and chaos can cause us to lose sight of what truly matters. Then again, it can make us feel overwhelmed with the issues of life, and at some point, we must make a declaration similar to what God is saying now: *Enough is Enough.*

The *Enough is Enough* stance requires courage, conviction, and unwavering faith. Still, it may cause people to want to play dirty to distract us or make us out to be liars. Here me and hear me well: When they play dirty, we can say with Divine Authority from the Heavenly of Heavens, *Enough is Enough* while playing cleanly with the Spirit of the Lord on our side without becoming shady, evil, or rude. Here is the scripture to recite: "*Through You we will push down our enemies; through Your name we will trample those who rise up against us. For I will not trust in my bow, nor shall my sword save me. But You have saved us from our enemies, and have put to shame those who hated us.*" Psalm 44:5-7.

How can we authentically love those who hate, use, abuse, despise, or talk about us? We need the presence of the Holy Trinity involved, period. Approaching negativity without God Almighty is a recipe for disaster. Without Him, we do not know what or who He is using to BLESS us, and if we block ourselves, then we cannot blame Him.

Spiritual Interdependence can change the trajectory of our lives, even if we are unliked, unwanted, ostracized, or black-sheeped. How does this help us, especially being the outcasts? It helps us maintain the bonds of love within our human psyche, preventing an uprising from within and allowing us to help ourselves and others proactively.

On the other hand, regardless of what we are going through or have been through, it does not benefit us to hate, abuse, misuse, or engage in debauched behaviors, thoughts, or beliefs. Why would it not benefit us, primarily if it is well deserved? Unfortunately, it creates Spiritual Taboos, *Mud Pies*, and generational curses with seeds reproducing after their own kind.

Reversing Mud Pies

According to the Heavenly of Heavens, it behooves us to use the Fruits of the Spirit to change the trajectory of our Bloodline or *Mud Pies*, especially if we have fallen short or want to stand tall in the Kingdom of God.

Here is what we must know about *How To Please God* and why we need to *Reverse Mud Pies*: "*But above all these things put on love, which is the bond of perfection. And let the peace of God rule in your hearts, to which also you were called in one body; and be thankful. Let the word of Christ dwell in you richly in all wisdom, teaching and admonishing one another in psalms and hymns and spiritual songs, singing with grace in your hearts to the Lord. And whatever you do in word or deed, do all in the name of the Lord Jesus, giving thanks to God the Father through Him."* Colossians 3:14-17.

Why does it take all of this to *Reverse Mud Pies*? Unfortunately, if we do not redirect our hearts back to God, our ability to make headway will become short-lived, short-circuited, or self-sabotaged. Why would this happen as Believers? When God has provided a way to UNITE, *As It Pleases Him*, our hidden, ungoverned, or uncorrected biases, thoughts, and beliefs will block our Spiritual Eyes, Ears, and Voice from conveying love and righteousness. Instead, cynicism, arrogance, and pride will take over, causing discontentment among those not Spiritually Versed in exhibiting Christ-like Character. But more importantly, we will begin to fight against ourselves while reflecting and displaying our struggles outwardly.

Why are our struggles continuing, especially when trying to do the right things while the wrong things keep happening? Frankly, if we misbehave with a horrific attitude and a negative mindset, is this not a reflection of who we are from the inside out? Absolutely. Regardless of how we sugarcoat our behaviors, if it is muddy, we will get dirt and mud on the people, places, and things around us, period!

With *Spiritual Interdependence* or not, who wants to be on a team with someone always slinging *Mud Pies* without remorse or a conscience? No one in their right mind would enjoy being hammered by *Mud Pies*; even kids who enjoy playing in the mud do not like to be hit in the face with it. Mass manipulation makes it easy to justify our behaviors, establishing our independent motives, where mud does not look like what it is until we 'get got' with what we did not see coming. Yet, it disguises itself in plain sight.

How are *Mud Pies* relevant in our lives today? It has become easier than ever to lie to ourselves and others about what we are doing, conceal who we are doing it with, downplay what we are avoiding, silently compete against others, or outright hide our motives through deceptive measures while proclaiming to be a team player with a foe mentality.

In or out of the Kingdom, regardless of where we are in life, how we feel, what we are doing, or our reasons why, being a team player has its rules. If we do not know the rules, if we are not in complete control of our emotions, if we are not able to properly govern our thoughts, if we are not a good team player, or if we cannot deal with loss, our Winner's Mentality, *As It Pleases God*, can become compromised. Why do we become compromised? We will settle for defeat amid a Divine Lesson, Training, or Unveiling for temporary comfort or due to hurt feelings.

When dealing with Spiritual Rules, to streamline our motives when playing clean or dirty, we must use the Fruits of the Spirit to change a negative mindset to a positive one, *As It Pleases God*.

What is the purpose of streamlining as Believers? It helps us behave Christlike to develop a Win-Win Mindset, uprooting negative seeds designed to hinder our walk with our Heavenly Father while keeping our mouths closed. More importantly, keeping our composure allows us to reverse negatives into positives, processing or rejecting information without giving the enemy room to penetrate, sift, yoke, or blindside us with *Mud Pies*.

Outside of what God allows to make us better, stronger, wiser, and well-equipped according to our Predestined Blueprinted Purpose, our responsibility is to put on the Whole Armor of God to withstand the enemy's wiles. To reverse any form of negativity from the inside out, we must create a Spiritual Bond with our Heavenly Father. While simultaneously using the Word of God as a *Spiritual Interdependent* binding agreement or Spiritual Weapon in *Reversing Mud Pies*.

For example, if we have a problem with *anxiety*, here is how to *Reverse this Mud Pie*: I cast down the Spirit of ANXIETY, and

I replace it with the Spirit of PEACE and CALMNESS. The *"Anxiety in a man's heart weighs it down, but an encouraging word makes it glad."* Proverbs 12:25. *"I will not be anxious about anything, but in every situation, by prayer and petition, with thanksgiving, I present my requests to God. And the peace of God, which transcends all understanding, will guard my heart and my mind in Christ Jesus."* Philippians 4:6-7.

For someone having an issue with *humility*, here is how to *Reverse this Mud Pie*: I cast down the Spirit of ARROGANCE, and I replace it with the Spirit of HUMILITY and HONOR. For Lord, Your word says, *"A person's pride will bring about his downfall, but the humble in spirit will gain honor."* Proverbs 29:23.

For someone having an issue with *confidence*, here is how to *Reverse this Mud Pie*: I cast down the Spirit of CYNICISM, and I replace it with the Spirit of CONFIDENCE and TRUST. I will *"Be strong and courageous. I will not be afraid; I will not be discouraged, for the LORD my God will be with me wherever I go."* Joshua 1:19. Because *"With God, all things are possible!"* Matthew 19:26.

For someone having an issue with *authenticity*, here is how to *Reverse this Mud Pie*: I cast down the Spirit of being FAKE, and I replace it with the Spirit of ORIGINALITY, GENUINENESS, and CONFIDENCE. I will *"Let love be without hypocrisy, I will detest what is evil and cling to what is good."* Romans 12:9.

For someone having an issue with *lying*, here is how to *Reverse this Mud Pie*: I cast down the Spirit of being LIED TO, LIED ON, or lying to myself, and I replace it with the Spirit of TRUTH, RIGHTEOUSNESS, and JUSTICE. *"Therefore, I will not fear, for God is with me; I will not be dismayed, for You are my God. You will strengthen and help me; and You will uphold me with Your righteous right hand."* Isaiah 41:10. For Lord, *"It is You who arms me with strength and makes my way perfect."* Psalm 18:32.

Align or Misalign

The Wisdom of our Forefathers provided the Legacy of information to fine-tune us Mentally, Physically, Emotionally, and Spiritually. Yet, for some odd reason, we have lost our way while overlooking the true craftsmanship hidden within the Word of God.

We are mere VESSELS used to accomplish a specific PURPOSE for our Heaven on Earth Experience with options. What are the options? In the Eye of God, there are two: ALIGN or MISALIGN.

- ☐ Align with the REASON for our being while becoming grateful.

- ☐ Misalign with the REASON for our being while becoming ungrateful.

In its simplest form, we are in Purpose on purpose or out of Purpose on purpose. There is no such thing as being in between Divine Purpose; however, when dealing with our own reasonings of purpose, it is possible to straddle the fence.

Unfortunately, it is the straddling that becomes displeasing to God. Why is He displeased when we have free will to do whatever, with whomever? Most often, when we are exercising free will, we are still in His face begging, trying to prostitute Him or pimp Him out. The moment something goes awry, there we go playing the victim right in His face as if He cannot see us for who we are and what we are doing.

Spiritually Speaking, we can become swept away by foolery while appearing wise in our own eyes. If someone proclaims to be joyful amid their misalignment with God or their Divine Blueprint, their joyousness is a lie. Really? Yes, really!

Joy from within, *As It Pleases God*, is linked to the Fruits of the Spirit, to bring us in Purpose on purpose according to our

Predestined Blueprint. We need the help of the Holy Spirit and the Blood of Jesus to cover us as Spiritual Atonement, building our *Spiritual Interdependency*. Without it, the human psyche remains in control, zapping our joy and replacing it with a Spiritual Void. Unfortunately, it goes overlooked time and time again because we do not know this; we are not taught it, nor do we understand how it works with the Mind, Body, Soul, and Spirit. As a result of not knowing how they are interconnected, we become confused, thinking happiness is joy and joy is happiness.

According to the Heavenly of Heavens, joy is intangible from within the human psyche, predicated on possessing other Fruits of the Spirit or at least becoming a work-in-progress while using them. Happiness is expressed outside of us with tangible people, places, and things, needing zero fruits, principles, standards, or know-how; it is free for all. Although we can have both, we must add the Holy Trinity into the equational efforts to obtain Spiritual Balance, keeping the psyche from leaning more toward folly than righteousness.

On the other hand, when leaving the Holy Trinity out, we can have one (happiness) and long for the other (joy), filling it in with something or someone else for a temporary fix. Is this fair? Absolutely! For this reason, the Spiritual Elites are given this for our Spiritual Knowing: *"By their fruits you will know them."* Matthew 7:20.

We are not given Spiritual Fruits to pass judgment; it is for knowing what and who we are dealing with, not mistreating or calling them out. They already know who they are; they do not need us to tell them. They are banking on us not knowing, and the moment we lose self-control, most often with our tongues or behaviors in the gathering or data collection phase, we 'get got' royally.

Why do we 'get got,' especially when they approach us with foolery or deceptive measures? Because we became a thorn or thistle amid the encounter, becoming no better than them. Is this Biblically specific? *"Beware of false prophets, who come to you in sheep's clothing, but inwardly they are ravenous wolves. You will know them by their fruits. Do men gather grapes from thornbushes or figs from thistles?" Matthew 7:15-16.*

What do we think the thorns and thistles are all about? It is about our interactions with people. In the same way, we know them; they know us, but are waiting for us to get out of character or misuse our Spiritual Fruits, making our rock unstable to gain leverage. When *Spiritually Interdependent*, we do not have to respond to any and everything; we have the right to Spiritually Deflect with clean hands and a pure heart, staying Rock Solid.

Rock Solid

What does a rock have to do with our Spiritual Fruits? Amid *Spiritual Interdependence*, we are either in right or wrong standing with our Spiritual Fruits. And if we do not know what they are, it is time to get in the know. Why must we know and use them, *As It Pleases God*? Our Spiritual Stability is predicated on them, even if we are clueless. Here is what we must know, and why Spiritual Fruits are essential, especially when faced with Spiritual Warfare:

- ☐ *"Therefore whoever hears these sayings of Mine, and does them, I will liken him to a wise man who built his house on the rock: and the rain descended, the floods came, and the winds blew and beat on that house; and it did not fall, for it was founded on the rock." Matthew 7:24-25.*

- ☐ *"But everyone who hears these sayings of Mine, and does not do them, will be like a foolish man who built his house on the sand: and the rain descended, the floods came, and the winds blew and beat on that house; and it fell. And great was its fall." Matthew 7:26-27.*

We are known by our People Skills, hidden in the Fruits of the Spirit, and our Christlike Character. And if we do not use them, it does not take a rocket scientist to tell us the quality of our People Skills behind closed doors. Yet, the funny thing about it all is that we do not need any wisdom to recognize good or bad, right or wrong, just or unjust. It is embedded within our DNA, written on the tablet of the heart. So, this is not a difficult task for anyone to master; all we need is the WILLINGNESS to recognize the difference between positive and negative, how to reverse them into a win-win for the Kingdom, and *How To Please God*.

CHAPTER 8
HOW TO PLEASE GOD

Timing is everything! In the Kingdom, if we move at the wrong time, we become unsynchronized. So, we must continue to realign ourselves accordingly, calibrating our Spiritual Senses on a moment-by-moment basis. For this reason, we must understand the differences between the worldly and Godly systems embedded *In Him* and outside of Him. If not, we can become swept away by our senses, habits, thoughts, biases, and lusts, pleasing ourselves and losing sight of our reason for being.

In MASTERING *How To Please God*, when our timing is off, we are often faced with people-pleasing. But if we dare to gather the courage to become a God Pleaser, *As He Promised*, our lives will change beyond what we could ever imagine. Furthermore, we would not have to run behind Him, begging, pleading, wallowing, or pimping Him out. All we need to do is AVAIL ourselves to His Divine Will and Ways according to our Predestined Blueprint, and He will come to us, granting us a Weapon of Confidence seen a mile away with Divine Provisions.

What is the catch-22 in gaining Divine Confidence and Wisdom? The only catch in *How To Please God* is to FEED His sheep! Feeding His sheep, *As It Pleases Him*, will EMPOWER us beyond human reasoning if we can get ourselves out of the way. He does not ask us to control, manipulate, fix, or shade them, just FEED and LEAD them back to Him using the Fruits of the Spirit and Christlike Character. However, to get to this point, we must become Spiritually Trained in this area to avoid 'getting got' with good intentions, looking like boo boo the fool because we do not know who we are, or become an easy target for the enemy's wiles.

Once we MASTER the ability to do what we do, in the Spirit of Excellence, we are better able to keep it moving to the greener or not-so-green pastures to FEED and PRODUCE results, regardless of how it appears to the naked eye.

How is it possible to produce in famines? Our Forefathers did it, and so can we; we simply need to know it! Our Spiritual Negev (underlying provisions) will hide in plain sight; therefore, we must develop Supernatural Confidence, *As It Pleases God*, to align with the timing of the need or our ability to command it to come forth.

We often confuse the Weapon of Confidence with pompousness, whereas Spiritual Confidence rests in KNOWING without playing pretend. What if someone pressures us to become someone we are not or discredits us for being who we are? Once we know 'Who' we are and 'Why' we are, *As It Pleases God*, it relieves the pressure, and we can still hold on to our Spiritual Confidence, doing what we are designed to do. On the other hand, if we change who we are, like night and day, we have work to do.

How do we remain confident or characteristically consistent when unmet expectations are before us? Unmet expectations are the leading cause of disappointment, or better yet, pressured disappointment, to be exact. We only experience pressure when we are unsure, fearful, masking something, harboring negativity, trying to convince someone, or when our inner chatter is out of control. Knowing this, we can counteract the yoke, root, or stronghold before it negatively locks in on the human psyche.

Listen, if we have the desire to come boldly to the Throne of God, *Spirit to Spirit*, without having peer pressure and *As It Pleases Him*, we must keep this in mind: "*Owe no one anything except to love one another, for he who loves another has fulfilled the law.*" Romans 13:8.   With this Divine Mindset, *As It Pleases God*, what belongs to us will come, what does not, do not worry about it, and what is NOT of Him cannot remain. The goal is to keep it moving in the Spirit of Excellence, allowing God to be God and hold steadfast to the COURAGE needed to move forward one step at a time. Why must we focus on moving forward? The Lord orders our steps, and He has the Divine Blueprint that we must download, *As It Pleases Him* and not to please ourselves.

Unbeknown to most, the Ancient Principles of Courage tell us exactly what it is. If we take a second look at the word courage, for a Spiritual Eye, it says, Cour-Age. Let us go deeper; Cure-age means CURE the AGE or CURE of AGE— all hidden in plain sight. For example, we would not go to a newborn seeking a Word of Wisdom because they cannot speak, right?   Okay, here is the deal: Our healing, cure, therapy, medicine, or the antidote we are looking for is of ANCIENT origin.

If we take this further, according to the Heavenly of Heavens, *How To Please God* is ANCIENT. It is in our nature to seek newness, but what we seek is of OLD in need of AWAKENING. Suppose we desire Spiritual Healing from the inside out, like our Forefathers did. In this case, we must GLEAN from their Divine Wisdom or REGRAFT ourselves from their personable mistakes to maximize our *Weapons of Courage.*

Whether we decide to glean, regraft, or both, the Book of Judges 13-16 shares the story of Samson that we should consider. Why must we consider Samson, especially when we are not as strong as him? Unfortunately, this is where the

Spirit of Error or Omission comes into play, causing us to 'get got' in our moments of weakness.

For the record, God gives everyone a Spiritual Talent, Gift, and Purpose with the Spiritual Tools to facilitate whatever, with whomever. Although some may possess more than one, He gives us all something to work with based on our capacity level. Still, we must KNOW it to USE it without ABUSING it; yet, we must also know the Spiritual Laws associated, protecting that which is already.

Here is the deal: Samson's story is no different than ours; thus, it exposes his strengths and weaknesses to help us avoid making the same mistakes. Plus, it shows us what will happen if we let our guard down in a moment of Mental, Physical, Emotional, or Spiritual Weakness. In addition, it opens our eyes to reality if we succumb to disobedience or pompousness, especially when we have been Spiritually Marked or are on a Spiritual Assignment according to our Predestined Blueprint. When we know beyond a shadow of a doubt that our STRENGTH and COURAGE come from God Almighty, we should not want to play around, pushing the limit.

Pushing The Limit

Why should we not push the limit, especially when we have grace and mercy to catch us? Once again, this is how we 'get got' by those doing less for the Kingdom but knowing more about Spiritual Principles. According to the Ancient of Days, the Spiritual Net from the Heavenly of Heavens associated with Divine Grace and Mercy is not the same as normal grace and mercy. What is the difference between Divine and regular? It is the Level of Accountability. Simply put, this is similar to having a separate digestive system to process Spiritual Milk or Meat.

For example, one system can handle both, and the other can only handle one. Suppose the system that can handle both systems plays the field, overpowering, abusing, or manipulating those who can only digest one. In this case, it will eventually turn against its own system, fighting against itself. Blasphemy, right? Wrong. Unfortunately, this Spiritual Law applies to us all, just like the Law of Gravity. Samson used his Divine Gift of Strength to pounce on the weak, and in the end, he succumbed to a similar weakness, bringing shame to his name, and it was more than just a slap on the hand.

Regardless of how we feel, think, or believe, when we know better, we are required to do better. But if we do not know better, then the regular amount of grace and mercy will suffice. Is this Biblical? It is a hard pill to swallow; however, here is what we must know: *"And that servant who knew his master's will, and did not prepare himself or do according to his will, shall be beaten with many stripes. But he who did not know, yet committed things deserving of stripes, shall be beaten with few. For everyone to whom much is given, from him much will be required; and to whom much has been committed, of him they will ask the more."* Luke 12:47-48. Although some may feel this is unfair or abusive, Spiritual Chastisement from within is not something we want to test, especially when bringing the Rod of Correction of our own making upon ourselves.

When eating from the Master's Table with Spiritual Fruits, Gifts, or Talents, RESPECT must be given. If we desire to be disrespectful, rude, arrogant, or disobedient, we will eventually find ourselves eating from our own tables of selfishness.

Why would it come to eating from our own tables? We have free will to eat from whichever one we choose. Nevertheless, when allowing the lust of the eyes, the lust of the flesh, and the pride of life take us down, causing us to get our eyes gouged and having to tread the mill like a pauper, then we must choose to:

- ☐ Do what it takes to regain our right standing with God, *As It Pleases Him.*
- ☐ Remain in our condition to please ourselves or others.

How does choosing ourselves or God reflect having free will, especially when life happens to us all, and a choice must be made here? We can put a new spin on it or choose whatever we like, but according to the Word of God, there is nothing new under the sun. We just have different characters with an up-to-date plot, thrusting us into a cycle of déjà vu (repeat) pleasing ourselves, or out of it with vuja de (synchronizing), *As it Pleases God.* Is this Biblical? *"That which has been is what will be, that which is done is what will be done, and there is nothing new under the sun. Is there anything of which it may be said, See, this is new? It has already been in ancient times before us."* Ecclesiastes 1:9-10.

The Wisdom of the Ancient gives us the *Weapon of Courage* we need to move in the now. I know we are up-to-date with all of the latest gadgets and technology; however, we are so insecure and lost beyond what we could ever imagine.

Why are we insecure and lost? Our inner man has an unfulfilled longing for Spirituality; we do not have a clue about tapping into it. As a result, we turn to social media to fill in the void, only to find that it is leading us into the PIT without knowing why. As a result, we use pompousness as a superficial form of courage instead of using HUMILITY as a *Spiritual Weapon.*

To be clear, I am not here to point the finger; I am here to help us understand how pleasant distractions feeding our hidden biases or traumas can zap our *Weapon of Courage* without us realizing what is happening until it is too late. What is the big deal, especially when living our best lives?

First, we can lose the ability to use our Gifts, Calling, Talents, Creativity, or whatever, *As It Pleases God*. Secondly, we can become barred from the Kingdom until repentance occurs. Thirdly, living our best lives is a matter of opinion. Therefore, we must weigh ourselves from God's Divine Perspective to determine whether we are Spiritual Heavyweights or worldly ones.

What do Spiritual Heavyweights have to do with anything? We must determine what is more crucial in the Eye of God, Spiritual Accolades, or worldly ones. Clearly, there is nothing wrong with getting our worldly accolades to do what we do in the Spirit of Excellence. Still, we must ensure we are Spiritually Equipped to handle the enemy's wiles and the Vicissitudes of Life.

Why must we be equipped as Spiritual Heavyweights? We can become a Spiritual Lightweight instead of a Spiritual Middleweight or Heavyweight, as opposed to having no weight in the Kingdom. Remember, for our Heaven on Earth Experience, we are Spiritual Beings having a human experience. For this reason, a worldly whatever cannot break Spiritual Yokes, Bondage, and Soul Ties off us, our children, partners, families, BLOODLINES, or whatever. Nor can it keep us balanced Mentally, Physically, Emotionally, or Spiritually, *As It Pleases God*. It only makes us judgmentally unequipped, selfish, and aloof, leading us astray or snubbing our noses at others. While at the same time, thinking everyone else has issues, or putting our secret insecurities on others without accounting for our own.

Blaming others for what we are secretly doing or have done without exhibiting kindness, forgiveness, and mercy causes us to get a side-eye from God. Why would we get a side-eye when we are entitled to do what we want and with whom? According to the Heavenly of Heavens, it makes us unprepared to feed His sheep, *As It Pleases Him*.

The Seed

Listen, if God served us what we deserved, we would hang our heads down in shame; therefore, it is imperative to use the Fruits of the Spirit and behave Christlike. If not, we inadvertently bring seeds back to our abode without knowing it or being prepared to deal with them.

How can a seed follow us back to our abodes? Unfortunately, we give our seeds energy, positively or negatively, possessing enough energy to be matched or manifested, regardless of what we think, believe, or are accustomed to. So, it behooves us always to lead and prepare with positive, productive fruits instead of negative, debauched ones.

What if we do not prepare ourselves, *As It Pleases God*? As a result of our unpreparedness, we have to depend on someone else to do what we should know how to do for ourselves, then we 'get got' with all types of church hurt, false expectations, or disappointments. While at the same time, knowing nothing about repenting, forgiving, or our Predestined Mission, contributing to our hidden desire for recognition, respect, and belonging, feeding our idolatrous efforts.

Why is repentance so necessary? It allows us to redo things, learn from our mistakes, or seek redirection through AWARENESS and AWAKENING. When making willing attempts to do right or get something right, *As It Pleases God*, the Heavenly of Heavens honors it more than those who are complacent. Does this really work? I am living proof! Although my mistakes were many, and my disobedience was evident; however, I did not give up, regardless of the mocking, laughs, traps, mistakes, stalkings, threats, or whatever. I decided I was not going down without leaving a LEGACY of Divine Information behind for others to glean.

My Forefathers and I were given a Promise, and I was not going down without fighting for what belonged to my

BLOODLINE. In my *Spirit to Spirit* Relationship with my Heavenly Father, I found that if I make a mistake, I must become quick to repent, forgive, learn, document, and share, building or healing the next in line.

How does repenting Biblically apply to us? The *As It Pleases God* Movement was built upon this: "*I say to you that likewise there will be more joy in heaven over one sinner who repents than over ninety-nine just persons who need no repentance. Or what woman, having ten silver coins, if she loses one coin, does not light a lamp, sweep the house, and search carefully until she finds it? And when she has found it, she calls her friends and neighbors together, saying, 'Rejoice with me, for I have found the piece which I lost!' Likewise, I say to you, there is joy in the presence of the angels of God over one sinner who repents.*" Luke 15:7-10.

Here is the deal on how this Biblical Scripture works. Knowing what I know, I remove myself from the equation, interjecting the Holy Trinity to do what needs to be done, period. For example, I know nothing in my own strength; for real, for real. Therefore, when I develop my *Spirit to Spirit* Connection, I target ONE sheep to TRAIN and SAVE another with a Multiplication Mindset based upon the Law of RECIPROCITY. As a result, He gives me Divine Revelation for the Masses with Spiritual Seals and Seeds according to my Divine Blueprint. Unfortunately, with me, this is where many individuals lose out on the Move of God, moving in their own strength.

How can we lose what we are Blessed with or what is already? If layers of negative debris cover our Gifts, Calling, Talents, Purpose, or Creativity, it is like we have lost them, especially if we do not recognize or know what they are. Plus, if we are Spiritually Blind, Deaf, and Mute, the same applies as well. However, it is left up to us to remain this way or up the ante, removing the debris or blinders while regaining the *Spiritual Courage* to move forward with the Holy Trinity at the forefront.

If we choose not to do anything about this condition, we may miss our cue on when to *Drop Our Nets* and when to pull back.

Dropping Our Nets

Stepping out into the unknown and letting go of the familiar is one of the biggest hangups of the human race. Why is releasing the old for the new a hangup? It is hidden under one word called FEAR!

In the Kingdom, we must relinquish our own agendas to embrace God's Divine Will, *As It Pleases Him*. However, we must also understand that fear is not a bad thing—it is a GIFT. How so? It is our best survival mechanism; nevertheless, we cannot allow it to paralyze us by understanding it for what it is. Here are a few hindrances preventing us from *Dropping Our Nets*, but not limited to such:

- ☐ The fear of losing out.
- ☐ The fear of missing out.
- ☐ The fear of failure.
- ☐ Fear of being left out.
- ☐ Fear of not being good enough.
- ☐ Fear of judgment.
- ☐ Fear of not being in the loop.
- ☐ Fear of being excluded.
- ☐ Fear of being overlooked.
- ☐ Fear of not being prepared.
- ☐ Fear of regret.
- ☐ Fear of not achieving one's potential.
- ☐ Fear of missing out on other opportunities.
- ☐ Fear of stagnation.
- ☐ Fear of not reaching our goals.
- ☐ Fear of not growing.
- ☐ Fear of being stuck in a rut.

- ☐ Fear of not learning from experiences.
- ☐ Fear of not making progress.
- ☐ Fear of change.
- ☐ Fear of disappointment.
- ☐ Fear of criticism.
- ☐ Fear of embarrassment.
- ☐ Fear of commitment.
- ☐ Fear of success.
- ☐ Fear of responsibility.
- ☐ Fear of not having enough.
- ☐ Fear of mockery.

Some fears are real, and some are not. So, it is our responsibility to debunk them with scripture. For example, here is how I would approach it: I would ask the fear, 'What does God have to say about this?' Then, I would quote this to the fear: *"For God has not given us a spirit of fear, but of power and of love and of a sound mind."* 2 Timothy 1:7.

Why would I ask the fear and not God? I could, but I go to God prepared. Besides, why would I take it to God first when I have not done my homework? Especially when 1 John 4:1 tells me: *"Beloved, do not believe every spirit, but test the spirits, whether they are of God; because many false prophets have gone out into the world."* Most think this scripture applies only to people, but it is applicable to feelings, emotions, thoughts, beliefs, desires, traumas, and so on. In the same way that we test others, we must test ourselves as well.

Dropping our Nets is linked to obedience, commitment, and humility in our *Spirit to Spirit* Relationship. Even if we do not understand the rationale of what God is instructing us to do, we must be willing to LISTEN and OBEY.

When it comes to *Dropping Our Nets*, here is the story: *"So it was, as the multitude pressed about Him to hear the word of God, that He stood by the Lake of Gennesaret, and saw two boats standing by the lake;*

but the fishermen had gone from them and were washing their nets. Then He got into one of the boats, which was Simon's, and asked him to put out a little from the land. And He sat down and taught the multitudes from the boat. When He had stopped speaking, He said to Simon, 'Launch out into the deep and let down your nets for a catch.' But Simon answered and said to Him, 'Master, we have toiled all night and caught nothing; nevertheless, at Your word I will let down the net.' And when they had done this, they caught a great number of fish, and their net was breaking. So they signaled to their partners in the other boat to come and help them. And they came and filled both the boats, so that they began to sink." Luke 5:1-7.

When God instructs us to drop our nets, we must be willing to follow instructions. If we cannot hear Him, we still have work to do because we are Spiritually Blind, Deaf, or Mute. When dealing with such an issue, we must reverse or regraft the root cause of this condition. If not, we will miss the mark, based upon our own recognizance.

What does our own recognizance have to do with anything? We have an ongoing open case with the Heavenly of Heavens; therefore, we do not get a clean slate here. We are given enough time to work on ourselves before being presented with the same issue again in a cycle of déjà vu.

What is the purpose of having an open case with the Heavenly of Heavens? In the Kingdom, we must become agile enough to hear the unhearable, see the unseeable, and speak the unspoken, developing our *Spirit to Spirit* Connection for our Heaven on Earth Experience, knowing when to drop our Spiritual Nets and when to pull them back with dual obedience.

What is dual obedience? Simply put, this is similar to having dual citizenship, sharing the rights and responsibilities of two places. As It Pleases God, we must understand Kingdom Responsibilities and Principles and the Laws of the Land, while respectfully connecting them with our Heaven on Earth Experiences. However, listed below are a few tips to get started:

- ☐ We must ensure we are '*Just*' in all our doings, especially when crying out to God regarding our inner hurts, traumas, or abuses.

- ☐ We must be '*Careful*' in all of our well-doings, especially when claiming to do something in the Name of God, yet operating with foul maneuvering tactics of unrighteousness.

- ☐ We must '*Protect*' our hearts by what proceeds out of the gateway of our mouths. By far, this is one of the first steps in obedience and opening the Floodgates of Divine Wisdom. Remember, the loudest person in the room should not move us; instead, it should raise red flags from the least to the greatest.

- ☐ We must '*Govern*' our tongues to the positive, righteous, and just aspects of our People Skills without justifying the behavior of those who couldn't care less about the meek, innocent, wounded, or disadvantaged. For this reason, we must master the Fruits of the Spirit and Christlike Character to ensure we know '*What*' to say at the appropriate time, '*Why*' we are responding, '*How*' to go about doing so, '*When*' to avoid the path of the unrighteous, and with '*Whom*.'

- ☐ We must have the '*Courage*' to move forward, get in Purpose on purpose according to our Divine Design, and know God has our back regardless of how it may appear to the naked eye.

- ☐ We must '*Call*' upon the Power of the Holy Trinity to assist us, especially when speaking the Language of God or using our Heavenly Language, knowing we will be heard without a doubt.

- ☐ We must '*Put On*' a good face before God and behind His back. For the record, this is NOT a mask to woo people. It is an engrafting of righteousness chiseled into the fabric of our being, designed to reap the Divine Favor of the Kingdom, securing our seat in the Heavenly of Heavens. If we live our lives doing the right thing in or out of season, we inadvertently avail ourselves to become the '*Cream of the Crop*' rising to the TOP in due season.

- ☐ We must '*Focus*' on the Will of God, doing, saying, and becoming what is PLEASING to Him. In doing so, we must also know that if we give Him what He wants, He will protect us according to the Divine Decrees and Promises He made to our Forefathers, while ushering us into our Birthrights or Predestined Blueprint.

- ☐ We must '*Avoid*' becoming heartless or arrogant; it voids the *Grandfather Clause*. Why? God requires humility in and out of the Kingdom. Bragging gets us yoked faster than any other vice known to man. How is this possible? It is an outward manifestation of disobedience hidden under layers of worldliness, while trying to convince others of our worthiness. Unbeknown to most, this underlying snare keeps the human psyche thirsty, hungry, unmannered, and out of control behind closed doors. For me, I look for private accounts with men, not public ones. What is the purpose of doing so? Behind closed doors, the true person comes to life once we unmask, especially when we are called out on our folly or short-sightedness.

- ☐ We must stay '*Awake*' or '*Alert*' to all things. In today's day and age, we often use the colloquialism '*Staying Woke*' as a form of awareness. Regardless of what we use, it is necessary to avoid being torn to shreds by those appearing stronger, yet weak in the Eye of God. Why is this the case? Those looking to prey on or expose others also have hidden kryptonic secrets they attempt to hide by pouncing on another as a deflective cover-up. For this reason, in the Kingdom, we require transparency, period. Why? It helps to develop compassion, mercy, and forgiveness, not a cover-up.

- ☐ We must be willing to '*Confront*' our issues without sweeping them under the rug. When we rise to the occasion to deal with ourselves from the inside out in the Spirit of Righteousness, deliverance is at our beck and call.

- ☐ We must '*Disassociate*' ourselves from worldliness to embrace the Kingdom Mentality. It helps us to operate in righteousness without having the tangibles of life interfere with our Spiritual Intangibles. Therefore, we must protect ourselves from becoming enslaved by our senses, lusts, or pride.

According to the Heavenly of Heavens, the *As It Pleases God* approach allows us to Spiritually Seal our Divine Blueprint, Birthrights, and Blessing simultaneously upon entering and exiting our *Spiritual Classrooms*.

Spiritual Classroom

When trying to *Please God*, what if this Spiritual Classroom does not work? All this means is that we are in the WRONG CLASSROOM. Yet, this is not a cause for alarm. Fortunately, this is how God tests us to ensure we pay attention. According to His Divine Perspective, if one can recognize what is NOT working, one can also recognize what is working, or what will work to streamline our Plan of Action, *As It Pleases Him*. So, it behooves us to get an understanding to ensure we are not playing ourselves short with the lessons we need to learn, the necessities encapsulated in the lesson, or what it will take to break or reverse the yoke of bondage.

On the other hand, if we are secretly dealing with classroom issues within ourselves, we have work to do! Remember, when heading into a Spiritual Classroom to revamp oneself, we must RESPECT the Teacher of the lesson. Why should we exhibit respect without being in a formal classroom setting? Our lessons will often NOT come as we envision; it may be a package we would not ordinarily open. So, beware while keeping the Holy Trinity at the forefront of all things!

According to the Heavenly of Heavens, when the Teacher's Wisdom is insulted, they must step back to allow the Student-Teacher or sheep to reflect on their behavior. Why is this necessary? Silence is the best TEACHER known to man, bringing stability to the human psyche of the Spiritually Trained. On the other hand, for the untrained, it can also rattle the psyche, giving the mind time to reflect, analyze, act a fool, and deflect what one has already gleaned or ponder on what they are missing. More importantly, it provokes one to become sharper or duller by choice and not trade.

God has PROMISED us Spiritual Access to the Divine Tools needed for our Predestined Blueprint. However, we must be willing to GROW beyond our self-imposed limitations, conditioning, or biases by willfully stepping into the Spiritual Classroom. More importantly, with such Divine

Privilege, it cannot be taken lightly, nor should it be taken for granted, because we must PREPARE ourselves, *As It Pleases Him*.

It is in our nature to want the benefits without putting in the work. Thus, when it comes to the Promises of God, we must Spiritually Till our own ground, putting our hands to the plow, preparing *As It Pleases Him*, and not to please ourselves or others.

How do we go about preparing for the *Spiritual Classroom* or gaining Spiritual Access? Through our *Spirit to Spirit* Relationship with the Holy Trinity (The Father, Son, and Holy Spirit). With this Divine Connect, we can gather the Divine Grace needed to DO what most cannot, HEAR what most are unable to hear, UNVEIL what most do not have Divine Revelation of, SEE what most are blinded to, and SPEAK the Language of the Kingdom, penetrating the Heart of God and man, and so on.

Can we really penetrate God's Divine Heart? Absolutely. We can penetrate it positively or negatively, but for the sake of 'How To Please God,' we are going to remain on the positive side of the spectrum, avoiding His Divine Wrath. Our goal is to gain Spiritual Access to the Kingdom of God, Promises, Wisdom, and Treasures without having God frown upon us.

What would cause the Wrath of God? It will vary from person to person, situation to situation, culture to culture, trauma to trauma, and so on. Yet, here is what we must know in all of our well-doing: *"For in it the righteousness of God is revealed from faith to faith; as it is written, 'The just shall live by faith.' For the wrath of God is revealed from heaven against all ungodliness and unrighteousness of men, who suppress the truth in unrighteousness, because what may be known of God is manifest in them, for God has shown it to them."* Romans 1:17-19.

God's DNA is within us, which means we already possess the Spiritual Tools to do what is right in His Eye. Once He shows us whatever or whomever through our conscience, instincts, or however, we ignore Him, continuing in our folly to please ourselves while wallowing in lies and debauchery.

Now, do we think God will show up on the scene with a smile? Spiritually, the unseen Rod of Correction will show up, doing what it is designed to do internally, regardless of whether we are in or out of the Kingdom! Why would this happen, especially when exercising free will? It is designed to make us *Spiritually Sharp* because we know right from wrong, even when we pretend that we do not!

Spiritually Sharp

Listen, the Spirit and Word of God are SHARP, and I mean sharper than sharp. What does sharpness or dullness have to do with our Spiritual Classroom? When dealing with dullness, it is a phase we will all experience. It is not a bad place to be unless we make it as such. If we allow it to become a Spiritual Lighthouse or Compass, it can improve our lives. Here is the Spiritual Seal: *"For the word of God is living and powerful, and sharper than any two-edged sword, piercing even to the division of soul and spirit, and of joints and marrow, and is a discerner of the thoughts and intents of the heart."* Hebrews 4:12.

Why does God not make us sharp without having to experience dullness? Please allow me to counteract this question with another: 'How do we know what areas to become sharp at or in, if we do not recognize dullness?' We cannot because God did not create us as robots. We have senses, feelings, emotions, instincts, and a conscience to inform us when we become dull. Or they prompt internal red flags of danger to preserve our lives. Taking dullness out of the equation is like our body not being sensitive to hot and cold.

We cannot omit or dumb down ourselves, thinking something is wrong all the time, when we can use dullness as a Spiritual Tool or Weapon to pinpoint our strengths and weaknesses, as well as our Gifts, Calling, Talents, and Purpose.

For example, just because an ax becomes dull does not mean it is not an ax with the potential to do what it is designed to do. It only needs sharpening to prevent us from using more energy than necessary. Please allow me to Spiritually Align: *"If the ax is dull, And one does not sharpen the edge, Then he must use more strength; But wisdom brings success."* Ecclesiastes 10:10.

What if we choose to remain dull? We have free will to remain dull or become sharp; however, with our choice, we cannot blame anyone else. Nevertheless, let us Biblically Align this before going deeper. *"And He said, "Go, and tell this people: Keep on hearing, but do not understand; Keep on seeing, but do not perceive.' "Make the heart of this people dull, And their ears heavy, And shut their eyes; Lest they see with their eyes, And hear with their ears, And understand with their heart, And return and be healed."* Isaiah 6:9-10. In all simplicity, we must want it for ourselves; nobody can want it for us.

In the Eye of God, disobedient dullness is another story, especially when leading His sheep in this state. What is the difference when dullness is dullness according to the English Dictionary? We are using the Spiritual Dictionary for Kingdom Purposes. According to the Heavenly of Heavens, we must use dullness to become sharper with ourselves, *As It Pleases Him*. We cannot use dullness to divide, conquer, or scatter people, especially His sheep, to please ourselves.

Here is what we must know: *"For the shepherds have become dull-hearted, And have not sought the LORD; Therefore they shall not prosper, And all their flocks shall be scattered. Behold, the noise of the report has come, And a great commotion out of the north country, To make the cities of Judah desolate, a den of jackals. O LORD, I know the way of man is not in himself; It is not in man who walks to direct his own* steps. O LORD, correct me, but with justice; Not in Your anger, lest You bring me to nothing." Jeremiah 10:21-24.

Dealing With Gaps

According to the Heavenly of Heavens, we have Equal Rights in the Kingdom based upon our Predestined Path. For example, if God granted us one Talent, Gift, or Calling, we are accountable for that one. If we have two, we are accountable. If we have three or more, we are still accountable for them based on our Level of Commissionability.

For example, if God did not call a person to be a Prophet, and they are operating in such a manner, Kingdom Access is denied based upon their Predestined Blueprint. Blasphemy, right? Wrong! To gain Spiritual Access to the Kingdom, we must live our TRUTH, and if we are living a lie or filled with deception, we are only fooling ourselves. How are we fooling ourselves? We know when our inner man is unsettled, and if we deny this feeling, who are we deceiving? Of course, we deceive ourselves only to deceive others.

For this reason, the Heavenly of Heavens cut straight to the chase, denying Spiritual Access to certain Kingdom Levels or Platforms. For example, with all due respect, a person can remain on Level One of Spirituality because they have not come to their senses to stop lying to themselves and others, especially when they should be on Level Five. To add insult to injury, this person will secretly or openly attempt to sabotage or discredit the person who put in the work to be on Level Five. Meanwhile, they inadvertently continue to knock notches off their own Spiritual Belt and become duller for refusing to grow up, use the Fruits of the Spirit, and behave Christlike.

Unfortunately, the former Level One recipient becomes duller and duller, desperate, and operating beneath Kingdom Standards; they begin underhandedly using the Believer's

Takedown Tactic. What is the Believer's Takedown Tactic? Firstly, the wolves in sheep's clothing or dream killers use this underhanded tactic to block others from receiving Kingdom Rankings above them. Secondly, they keep others stuck in the Milking Stages of Spirituality instead of getting to the Meat by engaging in all types of foolery. Thirdly, they use other people's Gifts, Callings, or Talents to get what they want and then take all the credit, spit in their faces, or block their ability to shine. Not realizing this tactic makes them duller still.

How can dullness follow us, especially when we have it going on? If this is the case, probably, the people surrounding us do not have the guts to call out the dullness or challenge it. Remember, sharp is sharp, making others sharper. And dull is dull, allowing others to remain dull. For me, I do not care what level you are on; I come to make you sharper, period! It does not matter whether I am judged or not; the sharpness from the Heavenly of Heavens pierces the heart of man with a desire to tap into their Spiritual Reservoir.

When operating in dullness, using someone else's tools without tapping into our own Spiritual Reservoir, it can cause us to fall short, especially when we think we are standing tall with goods that are not of our own, contradicting our reason for being. How do we make this make sense and applicable to real life? Everyone has their own set of Divine Provisions for their Predestined Blueprint.

Suppose we use something outside of what has already been provided. In this case, we can find ourselves consumed with failure, discontentment, feeling unsettled, battling with an indifferent yoke, or plagued by a negative mindset instead of embracing Divine Greatness.

Regardless of where we are or what we have going on, the Promises of Greater are wrapped in our Inner Greatness, spreading outwardly. We simply must know it to Spiritually Capitalize on it. So, instead of using the Believer's Takedown Tactics, we can use the Believer's Buildout or Buildup Tactics to change the trajectory of our current Spiritual Status or

Level. Yet, if we do not know this information, we will settle for less outside of our Divine Blueprint. So, from my perspective, name it, claim it, and be about it, *As It Pleases God*!

How can we be about our Father's Business when we are not as sharp as we should be? If we are presently operating in dullness, it only means we have work to do to avoid becoming divided. However, if we are disobediently dull, our DIVIDE will become GAPS in our Mental, Physical, Emotional, and Spiritual well-being. What does GAPS mean Spiritually? It means we lack Christlike Character in our **G**ratitude, **A**ttitude, **P**erspective, and **S**ystematic Approach. If these four aspects of our character remain NEGATIVE, we are doomed to become defeated in the Eye of God.

How is it possible to experience GAPS when our Spirit is stronger? Then my question would be, 'Which Spirit?' Our Spirit and the Holy Spirit are different unless we AWAKEN ourselves to become ONE. Now, when operating, *As It Pleases God*, in Spiritual Oneness, it operates in calmness, not chaos! Not knowing the difference leads to many Believers 'getting got' while trying their best to do right with rotten or uncorrected fruits, knowing nothing about the Fruits of the Spirit, or behaving Christlike. Listen, being scattered opens the door to becoming sifted by our EMOTIONS; therefore, creating DULLNESS while allowing the distractions in.

Why do we not speak about the Spirit of Dullness? We are easily offended by someone calling us dull. Yet, I am not here to offend; I am here to eradicate the enemy's secret chokehold that we fail to understand, primarily when we have not honestly dealt with our own hidden biases against our own. This secret of the heart causes more Spiritual Blindness, Deafness, or Muteness than we care to imagine, even if it is temporary. Yet, this is all the enemy needs to gain entry or take over, placing an even more significant divide. Why? Because they know the truth while we continually lie to ourselves about the hidden issues of the heart!

What is God looking for from within us? He does not make it hard on us, even if it appears so. He has given us Biblical Examples, Spiritual Tools, the Fruits of the Spirit, and Complete Access to the Holy Trinity. All we need to do is use them. Nevertheless, here are some of the items He will consistently check for, but not limited to such:

- ☐ He is checking our level of *GRATITUDE*.
- ☐ He is checking our level of *MERCY*.
- ☐ He is checking our level of *COMPASSION*.
- ☐ He is checking our level of *OBEDIENCE*.
- ☐ He is checking our level of *SELF-CONTROL*.
- ☐ He is checking our level of *LOVE FOR ALL*.
- ☐ He is checking our level of *PATIENCE*.
- ☐ He is checking our level of *RESPECT*.
- ☐ He is checking our level of *SERVANTHOOD*.
- ☐ He is checking our level of *POSITIVITY*.
- ☐ He is checking our level of *TEACHABILITY*.
- ☐ He is checking our level of *ADAPTABILITY*.

When it comes to embarking upon our Blueprinted Purpose, we play by a different set of Spiritual Rules. For this reason, God will place us on a different Check and Balance System. For example:

- ☐ He is checking our level of *SELF-ESTEEM*.
- ☐ He is checking our level of *FAITH*.
- ☐ He is checking the level of *IDENTITY*.
- ☐ He is checking the level of *PASSION*.
- ☐ He is checking the level of *COURAGE*.
- ☐ He is checking our level of *ENDURANCE*.
- ☐ He is checking our level of *POLARITY*.
- ☐ He is checking our level of *COMMITMENT*.

- ☐ He is checking our level of RESILIENCE.
- ☐ He is checking our level of COMFORTABILITY.
- ☐ He is checking our level of LEADERSHIP ABILITIES.
- ☐ He is checking our level of FLEXIBILITY.

The world does not revolve around us; we are here to SERVE in Earthen Vessels. If we were not needed here, we would not exist. We need the Holy Trinity, and the Holy Trinity needs us; therefore, no one should feel unwanted or unneeded. More importantly, we need people, and people need us. When our Spiritual Gifting is called upon, we must be prepared and able to step into ACTION, regardless of what we are going through, have been through, or are currently enduring, period!

God is looking for those who are fully committed anywhere, anytime, or under any circumstances, with or without preparation or hidden biases of deception.

We always want to know *How to Please God*, what to do, or when. Well, the decisive step-into-action mentality to feed His sheep is one way. The second is becoming the Shepherd at a moment's notice, which is a prerequisite for those being used for Kingdom Purposes.

When pleasing God, why does God not answer every question? The reasons may vary from person to person, situation to situation, mindset to mindset, lesson to lesson, and so on. However, listed below are a few reasons, but not limited to such:

- ☐ He wants us to wait; the timing is not right, it is not our season, or we already know the answer is no.

- ☐ We are in a Spiritual Classroom or on a cycle of déjà vu.

- ☐ We have not done our homework, documented, or asked the same questions repeatedly.

- ☐ We know better but are choosing not to do better.

- ☐ We have not taken the time to search the Biblical Scriptures for the answer.

- ☐ We have developed a deaf ear to Him while doing our own thing in a state of rebellion, disobedience, or pridefulness.

- ☐ We ask amiss, wavering in faith, wallowing, complaining, or begging.

- ☐ We are violating the will of another.

- ☐ We already have the answer that we did not accept.

- ☐ We are not exhibiting the Fruits of the Spirit or behaving Christlike.

- ☐ We are outright contradicting Spiritual Protocols, Laws, or Principles.

- ☐ We are using Him as a psychic reader, pimping Him out, or exhibiting ungratefulness.

When it is all said and done, we must be able to deal with people with different personalities, issues, traumas, conditioning, perceptions, etc., without contaminating them or losing our state of peacefulness or Godly Character. Plus, we do not go through dealing with all of this for nothing. Here is the Spiritual Seal for this Promise, *"For when God made a Promise to Abraham, because He could swear by no one GREATER, He swore by Himself, saying, 'Surely blessing I will bless you, and multiplying*

I will multiply you.' And so, after he had patiently endured, he obtained the promise. For men indeed swear by the greater, and an oath for confirmation is for them an end of all dispute. Thus God, determining to show more abundantly to the heirs of promise the immutability of His counsel, confirmed it by an oath, that by two immutable things, in which it is impossible for God to lie, we might have strong consolation, who have fled for refuge to lay hold of the hope set before us." Hebrews 6:13-18.

Greatness runs in our Bloodline, and we must Spiritually Seal it by availing ourselves to it. "This hope we have as an anchor of the soul, both sure and steadfast, and which enters the Presence behind the veil, where the forerunner has entered for us, even Jesus, having become High Priest forever according to the order of Melchizedek." Hebrews 6:19-20.

According to the Heavenly of Heavens, working with less and settling for less are two different entities in the Kingdom. Blasphemy, right? Wrong! "Now beyond all contradiction the lesser is blessed by the better. Here mortal men receive tithes, but there he receives them, of whom it is witnessed that he lives." Hebrews 7:7-8. When dealing with less while WORKING with the HOPE for Greater, it is considered MORE in the Eye of God.

On the other hand, SETTLING for less when the Promise is GREATER is significantly frowned upon with a side-eye. Frankly, this is similar to the spies coming back with a bad report to the Children of Israel, causing them to fear the presumable giants possessing the Promised Land. And then, adding insult to injury, labeling themselves as grasshoppers in the Eye of God. After all the Miraculous Blessings poured upon them, their minds were still stuck in Egypt.

On behalf of the Kingdom of Heaven, whatever we need according to the Promises of God is already written on the Minds and Hearts of everyone. We only need to remove the debris hiding them. Really? Yes, really! Allow me to Spiritually Align this: "For this is the covenant that I will make with the house of Israel after those days, says the LORD: I will put My laws in *their mind and write them on their hearts; and I will be their God, and they shall be My people. None of them shall teach his neighbor, and none his brother, saying, 'Know the LORD,' for all shall know Me, from the least of them to the greatest of them."* Hebrews 8:10-11. What does this mean for us? The Kingdom of God is WITHIN!

The bottom line is that we ALREADY possess what we need to go TOE-TO-TOE with the wiles of the enemy; we simply need to KNOW IT! In addition, we must do a few things:

- ☐ Stick to our Divine Mission without deviating. If we need structure in doing so, get it.

- ☐ Make the corrections necessary as they relate to our hidden brokenness or traumas.

- ☐ Avoid the desire to compromise our integrity to fit in with the cliques.

- ☐ Fight the temptation to sell out or secretly prostitute ourselves for temporary comfort.

- ☐ Avoid creating idols out of people, places, and things.

- ☐ Avoid the desire to be like others, and learn the 'Power Of Doing You.'

- ☐ Do not become sifted by the accolades of men because we are all human, and we are all Gifted to do something exceptionally well. If we do not know what it is, it is our responsibility to find or uncover it.

- ☐ Avoid the desire to become materialistic, greedy, or ungrateful.

- ☐ If we make a mistake, we must own it and make the necessary attempts to fix it within ourselves first. The 'Fixing Them' is out of the equation...it is through our own fixing that we set an example or empower them to do likewise.

- ☐ We cannot become dumbfounded by the enemy's wiles because they are designed to take out the weak, period. Spiritually Speaking, *As It Pleases God*, we are NOT the weak bystander; we are here to take possession of what rightly belongs to us, nothing more and nothing less.

- ☐ Assume the position of responsibility for ourselves, our attitude, as well as our Christlike Character. Recklessly leading ourselves or others to the slaughter is a big no-no. It is one of the quickest ways to reap coals on our heads while imprisoning our souls in the yoking process of chaos, confusion, waywardness, and negativity to traumatize the soul further.

- ☐ We must become patient with God's timing; if not, we will miss the mark. It does not matter what people think about how our lives should pan out—it matters what we think about ourselves as it relates to the Mission of God. Listen, if we wholeheartedly avail ourselves to the Will of God, He will not allow us to miss the mark, but we cannot allow people to get into our heads to cause us to move prematurely. If we do, our lives will mimic the life of King Saul in 1 Samuel.

We will be surprised at what a little Godly dusting off and Spiritual Adornment can do. If one does not believe me, simply look at the life of Joseph in Genesis 37-50, who is a prime example of *How To Please God* amid whatever or whomever.

- He was secretly tortured by the inner turmoil of being laughed at for what God told him in a dream.
- He was rejected by his siblings, depriving him of the fellowship of family.
- He was stripped of his coat of many colors of Divine Favor.
- He was denounced from his Birthright, to crush his ability to take possession of his Divine Inheritance.
- He was thrown into slavery to stifle his sense of freedom.
- He was accused of a heinous crime of rape.
- He was thrown into prison to cage his creativity.
- He was discredited and used for his Godly Talents.
- Others looked down upon him to zap his self-esteem.
- He was forgotten about, causing him to doubt God.
- He was overlooked to circumvent his hope in God.
- He was traumatized by a life he was not accustomed to living, giving him a reason to give up.

Yet, after all of the atrocities suffered, did it work? Who knows how Joseph really felt other than Joseph himself? But I will say this, from my perspective, when his Gift was called upon, he came to himself. Unscripted, Unadorned, Unashamed, and Uncoerced, Joseph stepped into action. Finally, the Gift that God polished up in his time of enslavement and isolation drove out his arrogance, pride, cattiness, privilege, etc. At the same time, He ushered in the Fruits of the Spirit to allow his Divine Gift to make room for him, setting Him before men in high places, and saving his people.

Developing Our Conscience

God is looking for a Reformation of our Conscience, not ritualistic behaviors! Why? Let me counteract this question with another: 'What is the purpose of going through the rituals and treating God's sheep like junkyard dogs?' Operating in the Kingdom without a conscience is unacceptable. God frowns upon hatefulness, rudeness, jealousy, envy, coveting, debauchery, unforgiveness, pride, and many other negative characteristics.

Then again, we proclaim Godliness when He is nowhere in sight, when we are beating up our neighbor with the Bible, especially when we are dealing with the same issues under a different label. Come on; we have to do better than this!

Here is what we need to know: *"Then indeed, even the first covenant had ordinances of divine service and the earthly sanctuary. For a tabernacle was prepared: the first part, in which was the lampstand, the table, and the showbread, which is called the sanctuary; and behind the second veil, the part of the tabernacle which is called the Holiest of All, which had the golden censer and the ark of the covenant overlaid on all sides with gold, in which were the golden pot that had the manna, Aaron's rod that budded, and the tablets of the covenant; and above it were the cherubim of glory overshadowing the mercy seat. Of these things we cannot now speak in detail. Now when these things had been thus prepared, the priests always went into the first part of the tabernacle, performing the services. But into the second part the high priest went alone once a year, not without blood, which he offered for himself and for the people's sins committed in ignorance; the Holy Spirit indicating this, that the way into the Holiest of All was not yet made manifest while the first tabernacle was still standing. It was symbolic for the present time in which both gifts and sacrifices are offered which cannot make him who performed the service perfect in regard to the conscience—concerned only* with foods and drinks, various washings, and fleshly ordinances imposed until the time of reformation." Hebrews 9:1-10.

Do we not have free will to do whatever with whomever? Absolutely! However, God will not bless our mess, especially if we have not taken the time to involve Him in the equation. Surely, if we did, our conscience would have convicted us of our wrongdoings, folly, disobedience, and so on.

What is the big deal about *Developing Our Conscience*, especially when we are a Believer? We are targeted! If we do not put on the Whole Armor of God, *As It Pleases Him*, in the moment of weakness, selfishness, anger, or trauma, the enemy will attempt to publicly disarm, strip, or deface us, crushing our faith, bringing shame to our names, and hanging us out to dry. For this reason, we cannot whitewash how the enemy operates, running our mouths with zero Spiritual Leverage or Power backing us, especially in a time such as this.

As a Word to the Wise, those possessing Spiritual Authority and Power would not voice it braggadociously; they just handle their business. The moment someone brags about how much power God granted them, I already know what time it is because God operates in HUMILITY, period! Is this not judging? For me, it is getting an understanding of what and who I am dealing with for Spiritual Enlightenment and to avoid violating my conscience.

How do we know the difference when their fruits are sweet and on point? According to scripture, here is what we need to know: "*You are of God, little children, and have overcome them, because He who is in you is greater than he who is in the world. They are of the world. Therefore, they speak as of the world, and the world hears them. We are of God. He who knows God hears us; he who is not of God does not hear us. By this we know the Spirit of Truth and the Spirit of Error.*" 1 John 4:4-6.

In all simplicity, check the Fruits of the Spirit, the Spirit of Truth, and the Spirit of Error, *As It Pleases God*, and not by man-made standards of power, money, sex, status, fame, perfection, and now, followers. If you do not know about this or you are using man-made standards, it is time to up the ante.

Why must we step up our game? I cannot tell you how many times people get me all wrong without asking me one question. What is the big deal? The Spirit of God that downloads this information for the use of His sheep is the same One who should download the correct information about me. If not, I already know that it is not Him (My Heavenly Father) feeding them that information, and they are operating in the *Spirit of Error*.

Furthermore, I do not try to convince them about anything. Why not? The PRICE that I paid to become who I am today does not need any convincing. Besides, if I have to convince them that I have the answers they are seeking, it means that they are not my Spiritual Tribe. I deal with KNOWINGS, period. If the Spirit of God does not reveal me to them, nor will I...I keep it moving in the Spirit of Excellence, doing what I am called to do, and so should you. Now, let us deal with *Overcoming Spiritual Error* to avoid missing the mark or our Spiritual Cues.

Overcoming Spiritual Error

At first glance, we equate *Spiritual Error* with making mistakes or being out of the Will of God. While at the same time, drawing dire criticism from those around us, especially from those who do not understand the Divine Plan or the Spiritual Training Process needed to facilitate or prepare us for our Predestined Blueprinted Purpose. Yet, in the Eye of God, when operating in *Spiritual Error*, it can serve as a profound catalyst for Divine Transformation and Spiritual Growth, *As It Pleases Him*.

Realistically, *Spiritual Error* is sometimes a Divine Compass filled with twists, turns, ups, downs, mountaintops, valleys, and sometimes steep falls. Simply put, it takes us to make mistakes or stub our toes to become Kingdomly Usable and to learn the difference in the Spiritual Duality of it all. For instance, we will not understand a valley until we have been there ourselves. Then again, we will not understand the view from the mountaintop until we have been on one. From every angle, there are different views and perspectives:

- ☐ We have God's views and perspectives, *As It Pleases Him*.
- ☐ We have our own views and perspectives to please ourselves selfishly.
- ☐ We have their views and perspectives to satiate an agenda.

No one is exempt from the different views, perspectives, processes, or exposure. We simply must know the difference and know what or who we are dealing with and why to confront our limitations or idiosyncrasies. If we do not know the difference, we can become our own yokes, playing ourselves short or missing viable opportunities.

In the OVERCOMING process, instead of merely marking our failures or errors as unredeemable, we can view them as pruning shears from the Heavenly of Heavens. When redirecting all things back to God, *As It Pleases Him*, they can guide us toward making the necessary corrections to learn, grow, prune, sow, get something right, awaken from our slumber, or become a better person. When viewed through this lens, our *Spiritual Errors* become Stepping Stones on the pathway to becoming a Divine Cornerstone, taking our rightful place in Kingdom Order, *As It Pleases Him*.

From experience, many people judged my mistakes, condition, or Battle Scars with zero mercy, compassion, understanding, or tolerance, as if God had abandoned or had forgotten about me. They did not realize they were operating in *Spiritual Error* by judging what they did not understand, by not asking fact-finding questions, or by digging up dirt to throw mud in my face to make themselves appear better, stronger, and wiser.

How were those individuals operating in *Spiritual Error*, especially when having freewill to judge, condemn, or spectate? First, while they were swinging it high and low with no shame, picking up all types of soul ties, yokes, and idols, I was putting in the work, selflessly building the Kingdom of God, *As It Pleased Him* to feed His precious sheep.

Secondly, in my Divine Overcoming Phase, the same individuals who judged, insulted, mocked, and spat in my face were the same individuals I helped in more ways than one. Moreover, they were secretly learning from me, unawaringly living from the Divine Blessings I possessed, and using my name for clout. While simultaneously gleaning Divine Wisdom from my Spiritual Reservoir with their foot on my neck, waiting for me to throw in the towel or give up on myself.

Thirdly, those individuals were underhandedly stealing and capitalizing generously on my ideas, thoughts, and ingenuity. How is this possible? They had capital and a team to polish and facilitate the work that I put in without them having to do much. This tactic allowed them to take my raw or ingenious ideas and polish them into marketable products, services, or concepts without me. In all simplicity, they had the resources to build a facade of legitimacy around my work, which added an extra layer of challenge to my situation, making it look like I was gleaning from them because they had a bigger audience and platform. Plus, no one would believe me anyway, except for the ones who witnessed it firsthand.

Yet, while wiping their mouths and licking their fingers, they have the nerve to insult me and the God I serve by saying, 'Why would God allow the ones working for Him to suffer like that?' My response was simply, 'You need to ask God for yourself!'

Why would they play in my face, especially when being built by the one they were insulting? They assumed they were more blessed than I am, because they were capitalizing and benefiting from me, while it seemed to the natural eye that I was not benefiting at all. Ultimately, I could see my Spiritual Progress as I was operating on a Supernatural Level. Nevertheless, they could not see beyond their mental capacity, traumas, and heart postures. Why not? Because of their Spiritual Blindness, Deafness, and Muteness, they were not privy to the Spiritual Insight or Foresight. In addition, due to the comparison of material gain, using money as their leverage, and operating in *Spiritual Error*, they were not able to understand the things of the Kingdom.

Here is the deal based on the Divine Lens of Spiritual Duality: They possessed what money could buy while secretly stalking me, violating my privacy, and watching me like a hawk regarding non-public information to break me down instead of building me up. Unfortunately, this is where ambitiously doing their homework (paying attention or vetting) and obsession became blurred, especially when admiration and envy are intertwined in their pursuits. To the point where they did not see a problem with this sort of psychological troublesome behavior. Nor did they realize that the external markers of success do not equate to inner fulfillment or that their behaviors are pleasing in the Eye of God. Why not? It is due to some form of unresolved discontentment and distorted sense of self-worth, provoking a relentless pursuit of validation or superiority.

On the other hand, I possessed what money could not buy, avoiding the yoke of temptation and bondage. Also, pumping the brakes on all of them because the God that I serve proactively WARNED me about them. They thought I had no one to help me, while not realizing, in my condition with my

Battle Scars and all, I was truly operating with the backing of the Holy Trinity and the HEAVENLY OF HEAVENS on another level.

Lastly, as the odds seem stacked against me, there exists a fine line between inspiration to become better, stronger, or wiser, *As It Pleases God*, and seizure to oppress or downplay the Divine Well of Wisdom to please themselves. How do we make this make sense? They took my little to present as if it were theirs, undermining the integrity of the entire creative process while attempting to use or prostitute me in exchange for help or funding. While building on a shaky foundation of deceit and excluding me from the equation or from the table altogether, to ensure no one would know the Divine Source, God said, 'Not So!' As life would have it, by operating in *Spiritual Error* without corrective measures, He is turning the Divine Table in my FAVOR with truth and reconciliation! The bottom line is that this ARK does not sail without me...The one who put in the work to create it with detailed precision, *As It Pleases God*.

In moments of judgment, we can remind ourselves that forgiveness, love, mercy, compassion, and understanding are FOUNDATIONAL PRINCIPLES to avoid bringing the same things we are criticizing back to our homes or bringing shame to our names.

On my Spiritual Journey, one would often ask, 'How could I *Overcome Spiritual Error* when I was messing up royally?' Fortunately, the BATTLEFIELD of my folly and disobedience was my Divine Training Ground. Plus, I was Divinely Commissioned to LEARN FROM how I was treated, ostracized, laughed at, abused, and rejected to understand the Fruits of the Spirit and our character traits a little better.

So, let us discuss the real issue behind *Spiritual Error* that has deep and lasting consequences in the Eye of God. No pun intended, but we will be particularly Spiritually Targeted when we operate in fault-finding, ill will, wrongness, debauchery, contempt, without a conscience, or with judgmental biases, having nothing to do with God or His Divine Will. In addition, *Spiritual Error* will also pinpoint the misinterpretation of religious texts, misguided teachings, or unethical behaviors hidden under the guise of Divine Spirituality. Basically, anything perpetuating cycles of oppression and discrimination that lead people away from the Kingdom of God or out of Purpose will contain a Spiritual Target.

What does operating in *Spiritual Error* look like for the average person? For example, an individual who is a faultfinder and blames everyone else instead of assuming responsibility, while surrounded by foolery and rotten fruit, is considered to be operating in *Spiritual Error*. It could also be someone who will lie at the drop of a dime to save the previous lie that was set in motion, which is often referred to as a compounded liar or thief. A person who is quick to cover up their mistakes instead of owning their truth, or is quick to throw things together, putting little thought into what they are doing, can operate in *Spiritual Error*. We can also associate *Spiritual Error* with someone who has a track record of creating or instigating havoc and problems.

Operating under the *Spirit of Error* in the Name of God creates Ritualistic or Religious Qualms that are highly frowned upon in the Kingdom. Unfortunately, it leads to a lot of confusion, chaos, abuse, and church hurt.

To avoid the Ritualistic Protocols, we are now Spiritually Self-Contained with the Spiritual Tools and Provisions needed for our Divine Blueprint. Outside of this, we are on our own. How can I say such a thing, right? When we want God to BLESS us amid disobedience, folly, abusing others, or when we are stiff-necked, we are sadly mistaken. Frankly, God will conveniently usher in the Rod of Correction or the Spiritual Classroom to train us in Kingdom Protocol, Laws, and Principles before causing all things to work in our favor.

What if we are doing good things? Doing good without Him in the Spirit of Disobedience or operating in *Spiritual Error* is not good in the Eye of God. So, it is best to involve Him in all things, whether it is good, bad, or indifferent.

Why must we add God to our equational efforts, especially when we are messing up royally? What is good or bad in man's eye is different in the Eye of God. For example, when God uses a situation, circumstance, or event to train a Spiritual Elite for their Divine Mission, the nature of man steps in to cast them down with shame, drag them through the dirt, or make them feel ungodly. Yet, if they do not have the experience, they cannot STAND for the Kingdom in the Spirit of Righteousness and Authority with the Lenses of God. Nor would they have Spiritual Access to a Legion of Angels to Divinely Protect them on a level uncommon to the natural eye at the drop of a dime.

Why would God allow us to go through treacherous challenges? We will be Spiritually Tried and Tested before being Kingdomly Commissioned; if we fail, we go back to the drawing board for a repeat session of whatever with different characters containing the same Divine Lessons, Skills, Training, or Regrafting Elements.

The bottom line is that *Overcoming Spiritual Error* is indeed a MINDSET and HEART POSTURE. Without Spiritual Training under the Holy Trinity, here is what can happen to the human psyche according to Acts 19:15-16: *"And the evil spirit answered and said, 'Jesus I know, and Paul I know; but who are you?' Then the man in whom the evil spirit was leaped on them, overpowered them, and prevailed against them, so that they fled out of that house naked and wounded."* Is this real? Absolutely! It is as real as the oxygen we are breathing right now.

Hence, we should not approach anyone or anything without God at the forefront, without the Holy Spirit leading the way with *Divine Illumination*, and without having the Blood of Jesus Divinely Covering us as our Spiritual Atonement.

CHAPTER 9
DIVINE ILLUMINATION

Can you see, *As It Pleases God*? Do you view the people, places, and things of God correctly? Spiritual Enlightenment and *Divine Illumination* are the same transformative encounter with the Holy of Holies. Some may have more encounters than others, but it is available to all mankind. Basically, it is a heightened sense of awareness, inner peace, and a profound connection to our Heavenly Father, *Spirit to Spirit*. Now, some may abuse the system with a false form of illumination, but *Divine Illumination* comes with the proper use of the Fruits of the Spirit and behaving Christlike.

Before moving on, the idea of gaining insight is intriguing to most; still, there is a level of accountability associated with doing so. What is it? Violating the free will of man. Most often, we want *Divine Illumination* into the lives of others; however, we must approach it to gain access into our lives and Predestined Blueprint, *As It Pleases God*.

What if we omit *Divine Illumination* for something else? We can 'get got' or turn on ourselves without knowing it. Above all, we can operate in *Spiritual Error* while appearing right in our own eyes, or we will see men walking as trees, like the Blind Man of Bethsaida in Mark 8:22-26. Conversely, we may refuse the spit that is designed to open our eyes to reality or restore our sight due to our negative perceptions and biases associated with spit.

Of course, no one wants to be spat upon, but without *Divine Illumination*, it is in our nature to jump to conclusions instead of jumping into Divine Revelation. The way God trains, heals, and deals with us may not be the way we are accustomed to experiencing them.

For example, I may not look like I am Divinely Anointed, but my Supernatural Anointing goes everywhere with me to protect, teach, and alert me and BLESS others without me having to say one word. On the other hand, where I am rejected, insulted, or mistreated, I shake the dust off my feet while keeping it moving in the Spirit of Excellence as I walk away with my BLESSINGS in hand.

Why would I take my Blessings with me? I cannot leave them behind...I am here to feed God's sheep; therefore, if someone wants to be a wolf, I give them free will to behave in such a manner. Nor will I lose my Spiritual Anointing by playing dirty or trying to change someone's perception of me. Is this not a little arrogant? Absolutely not! One would never know who I am without the Holy Spirit unveiling it because I move in outright humility with the Fruits of the Spirit in hand while behaving Christlike.

Here is what I know: Whatever we need from God most often will never be adorned the way we envisioned; therefore, we need the Holy Spirit to reveal what we are overlooking, leaving no stone unturned. If not, we will continue to miss the mark Mentally, Physically, Emotionally, or Spiritually, while pretending we have it all together in the public eye, especially when the Eye of God is PRIMAL. What is the big deal? If we miss the tangible provocations of God, we will miss the Spiritual Cues of the UNSEEN! Unfortunately, for this reason, the Church has become a laughingstock with little or no Spiritual Power when contending with the wiles of the enemy.

For this reason, and to be crystal clear, I am here to do my JOB and get the information to feed God's sheep. So, I do not play around with my Divine Anointing, nor do I take it for granted. And, if I have to call forth a Legion of Angels to protect myself from the wolves in sheep's clothing, I will do just that with a *Divinely Illuminated* smile on my face!

What is the purpose of smiling? I smile out of gratefulness. I cannot lose my joy because I put in the work, *As It Pleases God* to keep my Spiritual Fruits in right standing with Him; thus, with *Divine Illumination*, that rotten fruit was not allowed to spoil the bunch.

The Understanding

What does Spiritual Enlightenment or *Divine Illumination* have to do with our fruits, or Spiritual Fruits, to be exact? When possessing Spiritual Access to the Kingdom, we must understand two things about the Vicissitudes, Cycles, and Seasons:

- ☐ They Are God Allowed.
- ☐ They Are God Blocked.

In the Kingdom, there is a Reason or Seed hidden in everything, even if we do not understand or like it, but we can LEARN from or amid it. For this reason, the Agents of the Kingdom are Spiritually Trained on how to CONTEND, not defend. What does this mean, especially when the Bible says not to contend with another in Hosea 4:4? In the Kingdom, being that we deal with the unseen first, we are trained to STAND on the Word of God, RESISTING the Devil, causing him to flee. It is NOT going about our Divine Mission, fighting with others about God, or jumping in the ring with them to lose our Spiritual Crown due to the lack of self-control.

Amid our Spiritual Access to *Divine Illumination*, here is what we need to know: *"For what if some did not believe? Will their unbelief make the faithfulness of God without effect? Certainly not! Indeed, let God be true but every man a liar. As it is written: "That You may be justified in Your words, and may overcome when You are judged."* Romans 3:3-4.

We are called to live by EXAMPLE; therefore, once again, we must become Spiritually Trained on Kingdom Protocols, Laws, and Principles through the Vicissitudes, Cycles, and Seasons of Life. God can take care of Himself, and He wants us to TAKE CARE OF and FEED His sheep, *As It Pleases Him!*

Why is *Divine Illumination* so important in the Eye of God? We, in our own strength, cannot determine the needs of His sheep; He must transfer the *Divine Illumination* with the Spiritual Knowledge, Understanding, or Wisdom to us through our *Spirit to Spirit* Connection to know what needs are on the table or presently relevant. Why do we need Spiritual Involvement? A word out of season can contaminate or starve the flock, leading them astray.

For me, without my *Spirit to Spirit* Connection, I would not be able to write on this Spiritual Level with such conviction and accuracy, pushing beyond my earthly limitations. More importantly, on behalf of the Heavenly of Heavens, without having gone through the hurt, debauchery, betrayal, trauma, rejection, abuse, manipulation, rotten fruits, and so on as my Spiritual Training Ground, I would not have been prepared for my Heaven on Earth Experience and Divine Blueprint. Therefore, I take nothing for granted while LEARNING and giving THANKS for everything. At the same time, gleaning Divine Wisdom on a Supernatural Level with outright humility as if I am on a TREASURE HUNT for the Kingdom or a kid in a cookie store.

Morsel of Goodness

Every morsel of God is so GOOD to me that I confidently relish in it, regardless of what the naysayers are crunching on or hunting for to discredit how I do what I do, and why. Here is what the scriptures say about what is good: *'Beloved, do not imitate what is evil, but what is good. He who does good is of God, but he who does evil has not seen God.'* 3 John 1:11.

More importantly, in the Spirit of Righteousness, I do what I am called to do, help who I am called to help, make the call I need to make, write what God is conveying, and deliver the necessary information with no strings attached. Suppose it is rejected, or they are too busy to receive it. In this case, they cannot ever blame God for NOT having the opportunity to possess what they need to become better with whatever or whomever. Even if they fail to recognize it or become a mental or emotional cesspool, running to and from as if God is not who He says He is, the opportunity was extended to them.

When the Holy Spirit and the Blood of Jesus have our backs, all we need to do is LEARN how to gain Spiritual Access to what is already Promised, *As It Pleases God*. Instead of becoming mushy with little or no self-control, falling for anything or anyone, or feeling as if we have no other choice but to settle for less, just ask God for *Divine Illumination* or Revelation about whatever or whomever.

Why should we ask God for *Divine Illumination* or Revelation? It is not mandatory. It is a free-will query. Still, know this: The most amazing thing about the Kingdom of Heaven, the Hidden Treasures of God, contains Spiritual Promises veiled to the naked eye. Unbeknown to most, they are reserved for those who take the time to SEEK the TRUTH while becoming a work-in-progress using the Fruits of the Spirit and exhibiting Christlike Character. Really? Yes, really! I will say this again: God is not looking for perfection; He is looking for the WILLING, TRAINABLE, and OBEDIENT, especially when no one is looking.

What I am sharing with everyone, we already know...I am simply AWAKENING and ALIGNING, causing one to REMEMBER! In doing so, one person's debris may not be the same as the next; therefore, we need the Holy Spirit involved in the matter and the Blood of Jesus as our Spiritual Sacrifice for the remission of our hidden or open faults.

To be clear, regardless of who we are and why, once again, we all have faults, weaknesses, issues, kryptonite, and so on. So, we need NOT point the finger but begin to Live by Example using the Fruits of the Spirit and become Christlike in our Character, building each other in UNITY. It is for this Promise that Jesus died for us. Allow me to Spiritually Align: *"And for this reason He is the Mediator of the new covenant, by means of death, for the redemption of the transgressions under the first covenant, that those who are called may receive the PROMISE of the Eternal Inheritance."* Hebrews 9:15.

CHAPTER 10
SPIRITUAL ACCESS

Are you good with giving and receiving instructions? When God speaks to you, do you hear what He is saying? When God nudges you, do you feel it? When you do something wrong, do you feel convicted? One would ask, 'Does God really respond to us?' The answer is, 'Absolutely!' He has indeed PROMISED to do so as long as we do not pray amissly or acclimate ourselves to idol worship.

Above all, we must fine-tune our Spiritual Abilities to understand who is speaking to us. Why should we know who is speaking? Our inside voice speaks to us, chatting on a level of our adherence or tolerance. The enemy plants seeds of thought based on our level of deceivability, doubtfulness, faithlessness, insecurities, fears, trauma, or naivety. We have outside influences based on our insecurities, vulnerabilities, conditioning, biases, and so on. And then, we have the Voice of God, which needs our Spiritual Eyes, Ears, and Language quickened toward Him. All of which governs our *Spiritual Access* or Denial.

We as humans have a lot of speaking going on simultaneously; however, we need Spiritual Discernment to filter in or out whatever or whomever. What is the purpose of having a Spiritual Filter? It will vary from person to person, depending upon various reasons; *"But if you have bitter envy and self-seeking in your hearts, do not boast and lie against the truth. This wisdom does not descend from above, but is earthly, sensual, demonic. For where envy and self-seeking exist, confusion and every evil thing are there."* James 3:14-16.

According to the Heavenly of Heavens, we can become overwhelmed, manipulated, or confused, thwarting our perception or scattering our Divine Revelations without having Spiritual Filters in place. The moment we find ourselves all over the place or Spiritually Bouncing around, confusing God's sheep, there is a slight indication of unsurety from within or a fear of not meeting up to the standards set before us. To be clear, this does not make us unusable in the Kingdom; it is only an indication of the need for Spiritual Structure to build Divine Clarity when conveying, understanding, or filtering.

When dealing with *Spiritual Access* the way God intended, here is what we need to know according to the Word of God. *"Therefore, having been justified by faith, we have peace with God through our Lord Jesus Christ, through whom also we have access by faith into this grace in which we stand, and rejoice in hope of the glory of God. And not only that, but we also glory in tribulations, knowing that tribulation produces perseverance; and perseverance, character; and character, hope."* Romans 5:1-4.

Contrary to what most would think, God is not difficult; He is strategic, systematic, proactive, and consistent. For this reason, once we understand how God operates, we are better able to Spiritually Access and Divinely Align, *As It Pleases Him*. For this reason, it is best to Mind Map our Spiritual Journey when we are ultimately confused about what God is doing until we become a Kingdom Elite.

Why must we go through all of this to gain *Spiritual Access* when we already have a Spiritual Relationship with God? Regardless of where we are in our relationship with Him, we must have Spiritual Keys, knowing Spiritual Protocols to enter what is SACRED, without bogarting our way into the Kingdom as if we are running the show. More importantly, it prevents us from hurting ourselves due to misunderstanding the Spiritual Expectations or abusing the Rules of the Kingdom.

Unbeknown to most, Spiritual Abuse is real, running rampant amongst us like a thief in the night, zapping our sense of meekness first. Why meekness before hope? Without humility, we lose hope by default because we are too proud to do this, too proud to say that, too proud to apologize when we are right or wrong, too proud to be seen with certain types of people, and the list goes on. Whereas in the Kingdom, we are all ONE.

Regardless of who we are, where we are, or what we think, humility is required in the Kingdom. Yet, it is overlooked because we are taught to command the things of God to get what we want without getting an understanding first. Really? Yes, really! Here is what we need to know if we refuse to grow up, Mentally, Physically, Emotionally, and Spiritually: "*My people are destroyed for lack of knowledge. Because you have rejected knowledge, I also will reject you from being priest for Me; Because you have forgotten the law of your God, I also will forget your children.*" Hosea 4:6.

Instead, suppose we were humbly conditioned to Declaring and Decreeing what is already written, involving the Holy Spirit in the matter, and covering ourselves with the Blood of Jesus. In this case, we will have the knowledge that what is good for us will come, and what is not will be blocked. What is the purpose of knowing this information? Simply put, we need to involve the Holy Spirit in our lives and decisions without reservation because He knows more than we do. As a result, we would have fewer disappointments and stress, preserving our sanity.

Now, for the sake of our *Spiritual Access*, let us align accordingly: "*Now hope does not disappoint, because the love of God* has been poured out in our hearts by the Holy Spirit who was given to us." Romans 5:5. "Likewise, the Spirit also helps in our weaknesses. For we do not know what we should pray for as we ought, but the Spirit Himself makes intercession for us with groanings which cannot be uttered. Now He who searches the hearts knows what the mind of the Spirit is, because He makes intercession for the saints according to the will of God." Romans 8:26-27.

Paving the Way

Jesus paved the way for our *Spiritual Access*, but we must do our part within ourselves, perfecting our fruits and character through inner growth and molding. Here is what we must know before moving on: "*And He came and preached peace to you who were afar off and to those who were near. For through Him we both have access by one Spirit to the Father. Now, therefore, you are no longer strangers and foreigners, but fellow citizens with the saints and members of the household of God, having been built on the foundation of the apostles and prophets, Jesus Christ Himself being the chief cornerstone, in whom the whole building, being fitted together, grows into a holy temple in the Lord, in whom you also are being built together for a dwelling place of God in the Spirit.*" Ephesians 2:17-22.

We all have a free will choice to stay on the Spiritual Surface with the 'yes and amen' demeanor, depending on others to do what we are not willing to do. Or, we can go DEEPER into the Realm of the Spirit to the SOURCE, downloading Divine Information from the Heavenly of Heavens, but we cannot approach God in any type of way.

As we become a Spiritual Vessel of God, according to the Heavenly of Heavens, when engaging *Spirit to Spirit* on our feet or in motion, we must focus on doing a few things, but not limited to such:

- ☐ We need to Pay Attention.
- ☐ We need Repentance.
- ☐ We need Forgiveness.
- ☐ We need Clarification.
- ☐ We need Understanding.
- ☐ We need Preparation.
- ☐ We need Obedience.
- ☐ We need Focus.
- ☐ We need Proactiveness.
- ☐ We need Diligence.
- ☐ We need Unity.
- ☐ We need Involvement.
- ☐ We need Shareability.
- ☐ We need Kingdom Mindedness.

It may take practice to do all of these in unison, but with a bit of practice or a checklist, we can MASTER them simultaneously, guaranteed!

Suppose we become too busy pleasing ourselves with zero time for God's plan or getting our lives in order. In this case, it will affect us from within. In the interim of dealing with our internal issues, it will cast reflections or mirroring effects on our fruits, habits, thoughts, beliefs, deeds, actions, reactions, biases, competitiveness, and so on. If not corrected, *As It Pleases God*, it will cause us to get an ACCESS DENIED until we come to ourselves or wake up from our slumber.

According to the Heavenly of Heavens, we must remember that we are all a work-in-progress, and we will all go through the ACCESS DENIED phase for the Promises of God. Why would God deny us when we are sold out to Him? The reasons vary from person to person. Nevertheless, most often, it is due to not being Properly Seasoned, lacking Spiritual Training, we are unprepared for the Spiritual Journey, we are ill-equipped with the proper Spiritual Armor, and so on.

Why would God deny us in such a manner? For this answer, allow me to interject this scriptural story about the ten virgins: *"Then the kingdom of heaven shall be likened to ten virgins who took their lamps and went out to meet the bridegroom. Now five of them were wise, and five were foolish. Those who were foolish took their lamps and took no oil with them, but the wise took oil in their vessels with their lamps. But while the bridegroom was delayed, they all slumbered and slept. And at midnight a cry was heard: 'Behold, the bridegroom is coming; go out to meet him!' Then all those virgins arose and trimmed their lamps. And the foolish said to the wise, 'Give us some of your oil, for our lamps are going out.' But the wise answered, saying, 'No, lest there should not be enough for us and you; but go rather to those who sell, and buy for yourselves.' And while they went to buy, the bridegroom came, and those who were ready went in with him to the wedding; and the door was shut. Afterward the other virgins came also, saying, 'Lord, Lord, open to us!' But he answered and said, 'Assuredly, I say to you, I do not know you.' Watch therefore, for you know neither the day nor the hour in which the Son of Man is coming. For the Kingdom of Heaven is like a man traveling to a far country, who called his own servants and delivered his goods to them."* Matthew 25:1-14.

Stay On Ready

According to the Heavenly of Heavens, we have everything we need for our Divine Mission or Blueprint. We still must become Spiritually Proactive and Wise about maximizing or polishing up our Gifts, Talents, or Creativity for when they are called upon. For me, I advocate the *'Stay on Ready'* Mentality because we never know when the sheep are going to stray out of the fold or when the wolves are lying in wait to prey upon them. And, if we do not pay attention or miss our Spiritual Cue, we may be held liable according to our Kingdom Notches or Level. Personally, I am not willing to take that type of risk;

therefore, I pay attention to the Leading of the Spirit, even if the sheep do not realize their lamps are burning low, or if I am the sheep in need of Divine Guidance.

Let me say this before moving on: I do not pretend to be more than I am; my lamp has burned low, burned out, and lost its flicker. Plus, I have gotten the ACCESS DENIED so many times that I can proactively point out what to look for and why, with outright compassion, forgiveness, humility, and mercy.

Why would I forewarn others who have not taken the time to Spiritually Till their own ground or who couldn't care less about the Kingdom of God? I do what it takes to feed God's sheep to obtain His Promises and Spiritual Covering for my sake, then spread outwardly. While at the same time, doing what I am called to do without reservation, regardless of whether I get my feelings hurt, how I feel, who uses me, who takes me for granted, and the list goes on. Once again, I do my JOB...in and out of the Kingdom, *As It Pleases God*, and not as it pleases men!

In doing what we need to do to enhance our People Skills, *As It Pleases God*, we must do a few things, but not limited to such:

- ☐ We must establish EYE CONTACT to avoid deceptiveness.

- ☐ We must paint viable WORD PICTURES in the minds of others, allowing them to follow along, person to person, and then sometimes, *Spirit to Spirit*.

- ☐ We must keep what we do, say, and become SIMPLE, preventing overcomplications Mentally, Physically, or Emotionally.

- ☐ We must REDIRECT everything back to God lovingly and fruitfully without hitting people over the head with the Bible.

- ☐ We must be KIND regardless of whether it is deserved or not.

- ☐ We must be willing to positively BUILD ourselves and others Mentally, Physically, Emotionally, and Spiritually.

- ☐ We must be transparently HONEST with God, ourselves, and others.

Listen, once we develop a *Spirit to Spirit* Relationship with our Heavenly Father, *As It Pleases Him*, it is not something we would take for granted, play around with, or want to lose. Yet, if one has never experienced an authentic *Spirit to Spirit* Connection, they will easily compromise, second-guess, dilute, or pollute because they have yet to establish the VALUE.

How do we establish Divine Value in gaining Spiritual Access, *As It Pleases God*? We must come into AGREEMENT with our Divine Blueprint, surrendering to His Will and Ways. What is the purpose of doing so? It is in our nature to take the easy way out, doing our own thing or the wrong thing, especially when we are in agreement with ourselves only.

In the Kingdom, we cannot show up when we want to or become lukewarm; we are required to *Stay On Ready*, fully equipped with the Whole Armor of God. Even if we have a moment of relapse, we must be able to suit up at the drop of a dime, becoming Spirit-Led, doing what we are called to do!

In aligning our *Spiritual Access*, here is a relevant conversation between God and Jeremiah: *"Before I formed you in the womb I knew you; before you were born I sanctified you; I ordained you a prophet to the nations."* Jeremiah 1:5. But more importantly, here is Jeremiah's response, downplaying his *Spiritual Access*, *"Then said I: 'Ah, Lord GOD! Behold, I cannot speak, for I am a youth.' "* Jeremiah 1:6.

How often do we play ourselves short without coming into Divine Agreement with God? It happens all too often behind closed doors or when no one is looking, especially when our conscience knows we were running to and fro, pleasing ourselves.

Unfortunately, when it is all about us and no one else, this is usually when our inner chatter has a field day with our Mind, Body, and Soul if left uncorrected, unrepented, or uncounteracted with positivity and truth. Why does this happen? Selfishness is the breeding ground of all other negative behaviors, thoughts, beliefs, biases, and conditioning, invoking a Spiritual Yoke or preventing us from breaking it as we ought.

Without fail, when we get ourselves between a rock and a hard place, we run to God as if we have always been an obedient servant, playing pretend or faking it. When in all actuality, we have the same opportunity of coming boldly to the Throne of God as the next man by outright asking Him this: 'Show Me,' 'Help Me,' 'Teach Me,' 'Mold Me,' 'Use Me,' or 'Guide Me.'

According to the Heavenly of Heavens, we open ourselves up to the Divine Revelations of God by humbly making our requests known or outright asking to be unveiled. More importantly, when proactively doing a checkup from the neck up to gain *Spiritual Access*, we must avail ourselves to Kingdom Prerequisites, even if we do not understand the relevancy. Here are a few items to check, but not limited to such:

- ☐ **A**ttitude
- ☐ **C**haracter
- ☐ **C**onsistency
- ☐ **E**ffectiveness
- ☐ **S**ensible Shareability
- ☐ **S**toryline of Authenticity

What is the purpose of checking these areas, especially when we are Kingdomly Poshed? Poshed or not, we must all examine ourselves on a moment-by-moment basis, correcting the correctable through self-control and self-awareness. Listen, God is concerned about how we conduct ourselves; here is what the scriptures tell us, *"For those who have served well as deacons obtain for themselves a good standing and great boldness in the faith which is in Christ Jesus. These things I write to you, though I hope to come to you shortly; but if I am delayed, I write so that you may know how you ought to conduct yourself in the house of God, which is the church of the living God, the pillar and ground of the truth."* 1 Timothy 3:13-15.

Now, on this note, let us move back to Jeremiah for a moment to Spiritually Seal the importance of character development. For Kingdom Purposes, firstly, here is God's response correcting Jeremiah's mindset: *"But the LORD said to me: 'Do not say, 'I am a youth,' For you shall go to all to whom I send you, and whatever I command you, you shall speak. Do not be afraid of their faces, For I am with you to deliver you,' says the LORD. Then the LORD put forth His hand and touched my mouth, and the LORD said to me: 'Behold, I have put My words in your mouth.'"* Jeremiah 1:7-9.

Secondly, God tests the Spiritual Alignment of Jeremiah's Spirit to Spirit Connection. *"Moreover the word of the LORD came to me, saying, 'Jeremiah, what do you see?' And I said, 'I see a branch of an almond tree.' Then the LORD said to me, 'You have seen well, for I am* ready to perform My word.' And the word of the LORD came to me the second time, saying, 'What do you see?' And I said, 'I see a boiling pot, and it is facing away from the north.' Then the LORD said to me: 'Out of the north calamity shall break forth on all the inhabitants of the land.' " Jeremiah 1:11-14.

Thirdly, God instructs Jeremiah with an ultimatum. *"For behold, I am calling All the families of the kingdoms of the north, says the LORD; 'They shall come and each one set his throne at the entrance of the gates of Jerusalem, Against all its walls all around, And against all the cities of Judah. I will utter My judgments Against them concerning all their wickedness, Because they have forsaken Me, Burned incense to other gods, And worshiped the works of their own hands. 'Therefore prepare yourself and arise, And speak to them all that I command you. Do not be dismayed before their faces, Lest I dismay you before them.' "* Jeremiah 1:15-17.

Clipped Wings

When it comes to Kingdom Access, God will facilitate the *Spirit to Spirit* Connection upon request. He will point out the necessary corrections, possibly placing us in a Spiritual Classroom. We will be tested regarding what we see, hear, and speak while ushering in Spiritual Alignment, determining whether we move forward or go back to the drawing board. And then, He will give us instructions for our Spiritual Assignment to determine the strength of our wings or whether they need to be clipped to protect us from ourselves.

How can a mighty God clip our wings when we are ready to soar? Here again, this is where we are deceived and brought to shame, moving outside of our Divine Blueprint and the Will of God. Unbeknown to most, this is the enemy's take-down method, turning us against ourselves and God. Not to point the finger, Adam and Eve wanted to soar on their own, and look what happened, we are living the consequences!

Listen, God sees and knows all. If our fruits are rotten, our character sucks, our people skills are atrocious, we are easily deceived, or we lack understanding of Kingdom Protocols, He will hold us back to make the appropriate corrections.

Frankly, I had my wings clipped so many times that I have lost count, but I DID NOT stop while giving THANKS for all things and LEARNING from everything, regardless of how it appeared to the naked eye. Now, here we are!

Keep in mind that even if our wings are clipped, it does not mean they will not grow back. It means we have more work to do to develop strength beneath our wings from the inside out, building our genuine Spiritual Muscles to roll solo in Earthen Vessel. Of course, we are backed by the Holy Trinity, but we must do our due diligence, Spiritually Tilling our own ground without thinking the grass is greener on the other side.

Here is what we need to know regarding the Kingdom Access granted, "*They will fight against you, But they shall not prevail against you. For I am with you, says the LORD, to deliver you.*" Jeremiah 1:19. What does this mean? We will be provoked or discredited by the naysayers. Still, we must value our *Spiritual Access* over a fleeting meltdown, reaction, or whatever while keeping it moving in the Spirit of Excellence in VICTORY.

Why must we PLEASE God to gain *Spiritual Access* to the Promises, especially when faced with challenges? Let me counteract this question with another: 'Why would we not want to possess what we already have?'

To WIN in the Eye of God, we must put in the work, investing in ourselves and Spiritually Tilling our own ground to maximize the benefits readily available to us, allowing us to grow and mature through our challenges. In my opinion, if we must go through something, we may as well glean the Blessings, Lessons, or Wisdom from it. We are in it to WIN, not to snooze and lose. So, get up, get ready, and use what God has already placed inside of you to GROW GREAT!

CHAPTER 11
GROWING GREAT

If we desire to know where we stand with God or in the Kingdom of Heaven, all we need to do is pinpoint our Divine Instructions. If they are documented or not, then we have our answer. On the other hand, if we do not have any instructions, we also have our answer. What does this mean? Either we are not listening to God, we cannot hear Him, or He is not speaking to us for a reason. So, it is up to the individual to determine which is correct, making the appropriate changes necessary to invoke the *Spirit to Spirit* Connection needed to understand, pursue, and possess the Treasures of the Kingdom.

According to the Heavenly of Heavens, knowing the Word of God is NOT good enough, especially if we incorporate people-pleasing into the equation instead of God-Pleasing! How can I say such a thing, right? The Word of God is a Spiritual Journey leading us and others into the LIGHT. Amid doing so, if we throw His Word out as a flash of light, it blinds the Believer instead of illuminating the Spiritual Path.

If we have a desire to *Grow Great* in the Eye of God, the goal is to paint pictures, allowing others to see what we are Spiritually Seeing. There is no need to go overboard impressing others with unpainted or unconnected *Word Pictures*, confusing the flock, or creating undigestible word salads, pretending to be deep. All in all, we as humans need an understanding, knowing the *What, When, Where, How, Why,* and with *Whom* before moving to the next *Word Picture.*

Why do we need to master creating word pictures? According to our Divine DNA, we secretly or openly look for the win-wins, benefits, or takeaways. If the psyche is NOT convinced, at rest, or blinded somehow, we will secretly give a side-eye, provoking deeper thoughts or criticism, positively or negatively.

What is the purpose of understanding *Word Pictures*? God has PROMISED to Divinely Instruct and Guide us with our Heaven on Earth Experience with and through His WORD. For example, Jesus spoke in *Word Pictures*, making the Word of God palatable to the human psyche, creating an understandable and relatable flow. Now, some will understand it, and some will not until they are properly seasoned or ready. Thus, the picture trail was laid in a paper trail written in the Word of God. Comparatively, we should be doing likewise.

In *Growing Great*, if the spoken words are not moving the inner man, it is the WRONG language! How do we adjust it? Frankly, this is the reason for the Holy Spirit. Really? Yes, really! He gives the instinctual *Word Pictures* to use in our Spiritual Language to reach the unreachable, quench the unquenchable, speak Divine Wisdom to the already Wise, and so on.

Here is the deal: In perfecting *Word Pictures*, we must MASTER asking the right questions and convey the correct answers in Spirit and Truth. Of course, this is not an overnight process, but our *Word Pictures* become more profound in or out of the Kingdom with practice. So, it behooves us to use a Mind Map to help us create powerful branches of information when conveying it in its entirety. As a Word to the Wise, repeating this process over and over until

MASTERED makes our flow phenomenal, especially if we stay on the righteous side of the spectrum.

As a word of caution, if one conveys lies to manipulate, deceive, or prey upon anyone, we cannot usher in the Holy Spirit to canvas our debaucherous acts. If we do, confusion will meet us amid whatever we are doing, saying, or becoming, causing some form of turn-off, deaf ears, blinded eyes, or ungodly chatter. Therefore, Divine *Word Pictures*, guided by the Holy Spirit, requires obedience and humility, meeting people where they are. While at the same time, getting an understanding of the desired directions, organizational changes, or journey needed.

How do we know the difference between Divine or worldly *Word Pictures*? We can learn from both, so it is imperative to put on our thinking caps to ensure we do not reject our Teachable Moments. Once again, this is where our Spiritual Filters, Instincts, and Understanding play a vital role in the determining factors of what we glean or discard and whether we *Grow Great*, fizzle out, or become the sizzle. Yet, amid all, know this: *"But the wisdom that is from above is first pure, then peaceable, gentle, willing to yield, full of mercy and good fruits, without partiality and without hypocrisy. Now the fruit of righteousness is sown in peace by those who make peace."* James 3:17-18.

The Guarantee

In *Growing Great*, hidden within Spiritual Obedience, come Divine Guarantees that will naturally align with our patience and perseverance. People often ask, 'How can I place a guarantee, especially when we are all different?' Simple enough, my answer is, 'I operate through the Holy Trinity UNITED as ONE, *As It Pleases God*.' In this Divine Union and Blueprint, if this information makes it into the hands of someone, there is a need for it, regardless of whether they admit it or not. If they connect, they will receive, and if refused, it is okay. When they are ready, the Divine Well of Wisdom will flow more fluidly upon their return.

This Heavenly Information does not have a timestamp; it has a free will readiness one with Spiritual Contingencies. Now, if we want to add a little worldliness to the equation, it taints our Walk with God, even if we are devout Believers. Here is what we need to know about the Kingdom of God, but not limited to such:

- ☐ We must **MAINTAIN** a Victorious Mindset as an overcomer. *"For whatever is born of God overcomes the world. And this is the victory that has overcome the world—our faith.* 1 John 5:4.

- ☐ We must **BECOME** an unwavering Believer. *"Who is he who overcomes the world, but he who believes that Jesus is the Son of God?"* 1 John 5:5.

- ☐ We must come into **AGREEMENT** with the Water (Baptism) and the Blood of Jesus (Sacrifice). *"This is He who came by water and blood—Jesus Christ; not only by water, but by water and blood. And it is the Spirit who bears witness, because the Spirit is truth."* 1 John 5:6.

- ☐ We must **CONNECT** to our Heavenly *Spirit to Spirit* Relationship by acknowledging our Father in Heaven, using the Word of God, and ushering in the Holy Spirit. *"For there are three that bear witness in heaven: the Father, the Word, and the Holy Spirit; and these three are one."* 1 John 5:7.

- ☐ We must **PLEAD** and **COVER** ourselves with the Blood of Jesus for repentance and cleansing as a part of our Heaven on Earth Experience. *"And there are three that* bear witness on earth: the Spirit, the water, and the blood; and these three agree as one." 1 John 5:8.

☐ We must **BECOME** an Earthen Vessel for the Kingdom. *"If we receive the witness of men, the witness of God is greater; for this is the witness of God which He has testified of His Son."* 1 John 5:9.

☐ We must **AVOID** becoming a liar. *"He who believes in the Son of God has the witness in himself; he who does not believe God has made Him a liar, because he has not believed the testimony that God has given of His Son."* 1 John 5:10.

☐ We must **LIVE** by Example as a Testament for the Kingdom. *"And this is the testimony: that God has given us eternal life, and this life is in His Son.* 1 John 5:11.

☐ We must **VALUE** our lives through Christ Jesus. *"He who has the Son has life; he who does not have the Son of God does not have life."* 1 John 5:12.

☐ We must **USE** the Written Word of God as Spiritual Leverage for Eternal Life. *"These things I have written to you who believe in the name of the Son of God, that you may know that you have eternal life, and that you may continue to believe in the name of the Son of God."* 1 John 5:13.

☐ We must **ASK** Boldly, doing what it takes to **PROTECT** our Divine Blueprint, *As It Pleases God.* "Now *this is the confidence that we have in Him, that if we ask anything according to His will, He hears us."* 1 John 5:14.

☐ We must **TRUST** God, knowing our Spiritual Voice will reach Him beyond a shadow of a doubt. *"And if we* know that He hears us, whatever we ask, we know that we have the petitions that we have asked of Him." 1 John 5:15.

What is the purpose of knowing this information? It helps tame the tongue of man. How is this possible? Listen, as we all know, we can talk ourselves into and out of a Blessing. Yet, when it comes to the Promises of God, we do not want to play around, misunderstanding what is DIVINE.

Guarding The Tongue

In essence, when *Growing Great*, we want to be ever so careful about what we set in motion with our spoken words. As we all know, words have power, and there is power in our words. What we speak can shape and influence our reality positively or negatively within us, around us, through us, and because of us. Is this a play on words? Maybe or maybe not. Still, the weight of words can inspire, uplift, and motivate, or they can bring a strong person to their knees with hurt, discouragement, trauma, and a great divide within the human psyche. So, it behooves us to engage in *Guarding the Tongue* at all times, *As It Pleases God*.

Before we go any further, let us align what the Word of God says about *Guarding the Tongue*. "*Even so the tongue is a little member and boasts great things. See how great a forest a little fire kindles! And the tongue is a fire, a world of iniquity. The tongue is so set among our members that it defiles the whole body, and sets on fire the course of nature; and it is set on fire by hell. For every kind of beast and bird, of reptile and creature of the sea, is tamed and has been tamed by mankind. But no man can tame the tongue. It is an unruly evil, full of deadly poison. With it we bless our God and Father, and with it we curse men, who have been made in the similitude of God. Out of the same mouth proceed blessing and cursing. My brethren, these things ought not to be so."* James 3:5-10.

Growing Great requires us to guard our tongues and open our Spiritual Eyes and Ears to the Language of the Kingdom. Doing so helps us see, hear, and speak differently, *As It Pleases God*. Do we not have free will to govern our tongues to say what we want, when we want, how we want, where we want, and to whom we desire without God? Absolutely!

Nevertheless, how great is someone who has loose lips, sinks ships, and destroys people for their benefit and lack of self-control? Wait, wait, wait...do not answer this question yet. Here is one of the Divine Keys to *Growing Great*, hidden in plain sight: *"Who is wise and understanding among you? Let him show by good conduct that his works are done in the meekness of wisdom."* James 3:13.

Amid *Guarding The Tongue*, we must also pay attention Mentally, Physically, Emotionally, and Spiritually, ensuring we can glean Divine Wisdom on a Supernatural Level according to our Predestined Blueprint. Why must we pay attention to these other areas? The Level of Wisdom will vary, depending upon our Divine Purpose, Spiritual Tolerance, and Classroom Trainability.

We have this little saying, 'Do not let your tongue write a check you cannot cash.' Well, when dealing in the Realm of the Spirit, the same also applies. For example, if we are not well-versed or adequately trained in the UNSEEN, it will traumatize the human psyche more than it will help. So, God will not overwhelm us with what will frighten us or shake us to the core. For this reason, He will use stages and levels in Spiritual Transformation or Transitioning Phases while holding us accountable in these areas.

How is this example applicable to a Believer? When we misuse Spiritual Means, engaging in debauchery when we know better, the Spiritual Chastening is heftier than for someone clueless about Spiritual Protocols, Principles, Laws, and Violations. Or, if we play around in Spiritual Debauchery without understanding the cost of our actions, it creates a Spiritual Taboo as well. Unfortunately, this is how generational curses are levied on a Bloodline who are oblivious to the reasons associated, causing Spiritual Blindness, Deafness, and Muteness by default.

Once again, a man's tongue usually sets curses in motion with our actionable words (the words that make it into reality). Therefore, it is always best to keep our spoken words on the positive side of the spectrum, even if we are thinking negative thoughts or our mental chatter is off the chart.

How is it possible to remain on the positive side of the spectrum with negative thoughts and mental chatter? We have a choice of counteracting (replacing with the positive), counterbalancing (self-correcting, self-analyzing, or self-disciplining), or allowing the negative to remain without verbalizing it. The moment we set our words in motion or act upon them, we are accountable.

Suppose our thoughts DO NOT manifest on an actionable level. In this case, we can deal with them within ourselves without involving another person or allowing the seed to find soil outside of us. Doing so gives us an opportunity to self-correct instead of self-destructing by involving the well-being of another or violating their free will.

What is the big deal when we can say whatever we want, whenever, and however? If we are not Spiritually Astute, we do not know the Level of Anointing or Commissionability of the person we are casting doom and gloom over. Therefore, we can cause our negative words to find their way back to our house, ourselves, our family, or something connected to us. So, be careful with the tongue. Better yet, we can keep it simple by NOT saying anything we do not want to return or find its way back to us or the ones we love.

Clearly, no one is exempt from the SEEDS of negative thoughts, words, and mental chatter. Still, it is our responsibility to positively change the trajectory of them and repent, especially if we desire to receive Divine Instructions or develop a *Spirit to Spirit* Relationship with our Heavenly Father. Here is why we need to do this: *"For the weapons of our warfare are not carnal but mighty in God for pulling down strongholds, casting down arguments and every high thing that exalts itself against the knowledge of God, bringing every thought into captivity to the obedience of Christ, and being ready to punish all disobedience when your obedience is fulfilled."* 2 Corinthians 10:4-6.

What is the purpose of capturing our thoughts, words, and desires? We become what we think about or what we continuously entertain. *"For as he thinks in his heart, so is he. 'Eat and drink!' he says to you, but his heart is not with you."* Proverbs 23:7. We can determine who we are dealing with by their conversations. Unfortunately, if we choose not to pay attention, here is what happens according to scripture: *"The morsel you have eaten, you will vomit up, and waste your pleasant words."* Proverbs 23:8. In so many words, they will develop a deaf ear; however, it is NOT designed for us to react or judge; it is to understand WHAT or WHOM we are dealing with.

In the Kingdom, here are the instructions to heed to avoid becoming consumed by the Pharisees' Spirit. *"Do not speak in the hearing of a fool, for he will despise the wisdom of your words. Do not remove the ancient landmark, nor enter the fields of the fatherless; for their Redeemer is mighty; He will plead their cause against you. Apply your heart to instruction, and your ears to words of knowledge."* Proverbs 23:9-12.

What does this mean for us when *Growing Great*? We must take ourselves out of the equation, usher in the Holy Spirit to speak the Spiritual Language needed at that moment, use the Fruits of the Spirit, and behave Christlike. Then again, there are times when NO RESPONSE is needed, but GRATITUDE is a must, regardless of how it appears to the naked eye! Yet, we must know the difference, and it is through our Spiritual

Instincts and the Holy Spirit we can respond accordingly, ensuring our words are effective and on point.

Unbeknown to most, it is our responsibility to use our voice to raise an objection to what is unpleasing, unnatural, ungodly, yoking, or out of order to the natural eye with the Word of God while covering ourselves with the Blood of Jesus. What if we are clueless about Godly Formality? It is okay to be clueless, but we must be CLEAR about the intentions of the heart. We all have a conscience, knowing the difference between right and wrong, good and bad, positive and negative, light and darkness, and so on, even if we do not practice using it, ignore its responses, or have placed it in a desensitized mode.

In the quest for personal growth, *As It Pleases God*, make sure that you are *Spiritually Vetting* yourself and others to ensure the Holy Trinity is a viable resource in the equation. By ensuring your Spiritual Foundation is strong and surrounded by like-minded individuals, the path to personal and Spiritual Growth becomes more intentional, targeted, and focused on the essential elements of *Growing Great*.

CHAPTER 12
SPIRITUAL VETTING

Do you know what *Spiritual Vetting* is? Then again, do you know what *Spiritual Vetting* is not? In this last chapter on *How To Please God*, I am going to share my countrified roots to close this book with lifelong teachings in building the confidence needed to become who you already are.

How can one become if they already are? It is called EVOLUTION. For example, there is an adult in a baby; still, the growth process must occur in stages before becoming an adult. However, if proper learning does not occur in the childhood stages, one will have a childhood mentality in an adult body. For this reason, *Spiritual Vetting* is necessary to prevent us from becoming unequally yoked.

Spiritual Vetting is basically using our Spiritual Discernment faculties to align with people, places, and things that are for us and kindly weeding out what is not. Why do we need to be kind? In the same way that kindness is a SEED, so is unkindness.

In or out of our Evolutional Seasons or the *Spiritual Vetting* process, we will deal with two additional types of SEEDS outside of our good and bad or righteous or unrighteous charactorial SEEDS, which are:

- ☐ Seeds on the GIVE.
- ☐ Seeds on the TAKE.

What does this have to do with us? In varying portions or balances, we all have both governing what takes ROOT in the human psyche. We can give a little and take much, or we can give much and take less. And then again, we can give information only to fish out who or what we can take without giving back to the source. Therefore, we must become very CAUTIOUS about those who only talk about things, hoping someone will volunteer to give what they are not willing to give to themselves. Why must we exercise caution? We are dealing with a Deceptive Spirit, even if it is packaged pristinely.

When *Spiritually Vetting*, we do not want to become a user or manipulator. In the Kingdom, this is greatly frowned upon because the Promises and Blueprints of God from our Heavenly Father come with their own set of Divine Provisions from the least to the greatest.

How is it possible to have Divine Provisions when we are between a rock and a hard place? It is dealt out in stages or levels when dealing with Kingdom Capital, ensuring we can MASTER where we are before moving on.

Why would God limit us? We will naturally gravitate toward ungratefulness or unrighteousness, especially if we cannot MASTER where we are Mentally, Physically, Emotionally, or Spiritually. Regardless of what we possess or who we are, this character trait is wrapped in a typical package called SELFISHNESS. Unfortunately, when this becomes our normal, it goes unrecognized unless we constantly examine ourselves with the Fruits of the Spirit and Christlike Character to develop SELFLESSNESS, *As It Pleases God*.

In the *Spiritual Vetting* process, here are a few things we must understand, but not limited to such:

- ☐ We must understand God's Nature as Believers and our propensities in Earthen Vessels.

- ☐ We must understand the importance of REPENTING and the power of FORGIVENESS.

- ☐ We must understand the USE of the Blood of Jesus as Spiritual Atonement.

- ☐ We must understand how to become ONE with the Holy Spirit by AWAKENING our Spirit.

- ☐ We must understand our Divine Blueprint and our reason for being with a WILLINGNESS to complete the MISSION.

- ☐ We must understand the use of the Fruits of the Spirit (Love, Joy, Peace, Patience, Kindness, Goodness, Faithfulness, Gentleness, and Self-Control).

- ☐ We must understand the importance of exhibiting Christlike Character and displaying our Kingdom Etiquette at all times.

- ☐ We must understand how to UNVEIL our Spiritual Eyes, Ears, and Language to connect to God, *Spirit to Spirit*.

- ☐ We must understand the things God hates and understand His reasons why.

- ☐ We must understand the value hidden in obedience, humility, learning, and love.

- ☐ We must understand how to tame the lust of the eyes, the lust of the flesh, and the pride of life.

- ☐ We must understand the importance of doing a check-up from the neck up and examining ourselves according to the Word of God.

Why do we need to know all of this, especially when we are not under the Law? Then my question would be, 'What are we under?' Please allow that to simmer for a moment!

Frankly, this is how we are DECEIVED, doing whatever with whomever without realizing the Principles, Laws, and Decrees are WITHIN us, not subject to the judgment of men but to the manipulation of them.

Has anyone ever stopped to think about the reasons why we are so torn up from the floor up and from the inside out? Amid our deceptional state of being, we cannot tell anyone about the truth within the human psyche because if we did, they would think we are insane. You can keep lying to yourself if you like, but let me say this: When there is a chokehold on you, your life, your child, or whatever, the truth has a way of surfacing.

Playing Possum

When we violate ourselves in such a manner, the human psyche *'Plays Possum'* with us. How is it possible to align the things of God with a possum? Although a possum looks very strange from the south where I am from, they have powerful Spiritual Principles we can glean.

How is it possible to learn from a possum? They live their lives by Divine Design and preserve their Bloodline with what is written within their DNA Structure, even if we think they are repulsive, ugly, scary, or smelly. Listen, everything has a Divine Purpose in the Eye of God, and if we are not in Purpose on purpose, who are we to judge what is doing what they do best, right?

Yet, here we are, fighting over what is already written within our DNA Structure. But to add insult to injury, contending over who is right or wrong, especially regarding what is FINITE according to the Heavenly of Heavens.

Are we not entitled to our own opinions? Absolutely! Amid our lies and opinions, the truth is that we are the only ones within God's Divine Creation, fighting over the Genetic Codes, Principles, or Laws existing with or without us, similar to the Law of Gravity. As a result of the Spiritual Omission, we secretly fight against ourselves, our Bloodline, our Promises, and so on, to our detriment, without realizing what we are doing. Without understanding that no one is 100% right or wrong in the Eye of God, and we all have our own personal Spiritual Journey.

Listen, when we are out of the Will of God, not using the Divine Principles and Laws designed to save and enhance our lives for the better, here is the '*Playing Possum*' in action, but not limited to such:

☐ We operate with fang-like teeth, creating fear in those presumably having what we want as we allow coveting, jealousy, envy, pride, greed, and competitiveness to consume our being, traumatizing those around us.

☐ We tend to foam out the mouth when it comes down to the lust of the eyes, the lust of the flesh, and the pride of life, with a Spiritual Transfer of all types of Spiritual Paralysis, Recruits, or Diseases.

- We do not perform well in the light or areas of illumination requiring transparency. So, we lurk in the dark areas, fluently moving through life on our terms with our senses instead of our Spiritual Instincts. Remarkably, this all too common Spiritual Omission contributes to us seeing what we want to see, hearing what we want to hear, and behaving how we want to behave, thwarting our perceptions with little or no correction.

- We are easily distracted, traumatized, and blinded by sudden and unexpected rays of glaring light, causing us to become blindsided or confused by the Vicissitudes of Life. Or, we become Spiritually Yoked to the core for not paying attention to the wolves in sheep's clothing through the Word of God, the Fruits of the Spirit, or using Christlike Character.

- We become foul, nasty, or rude in our approach to getting what we want or getting rid of what we do not. Not realizing that KINDNESS and GENTLENESS help us approach any situation or circumstance. How can this help us? It assists in asking the appropriate questions to EXTRACT and CONVERT the necessary information to speak the language needed to Wisely Approach with caution, breaking through barriers most cannot.

- We pretend to be dead to the things we need, especially when deception is involved in using or getting over on someone for what we want. And then, suddenly, we become vibrant and lively, roaming about doing whatever, with whomever, when we are not questioned, challenged, called out, or restricted. In my opinion, this leads us into becoming a stiff-necked, disobedient, pompous, or rebellious person, not realizing the character traits exhibited until after the fact or deed is done.

- ☐ We play dumb or ignorant, playing tricks to fool people, or play the victim. The *Mind Games* of today have become so CAPITALISTIC, confounding the Spiritually Wise to the point where they must stay on Spiritual Alert 24/7. Why would the enemy play tricks on us? It is designed to wear us down, causing us to drop our Spiritual Guards to allow the enemy to penetrate in our moments of weakness. However, it is for this reason that it is imperative to operate Mentally, Physically, Emotionally, and Spiritually, *As It Pleases God*. Listen, if God is included in the equation, we have a Promise of Spiritual Leverage. Whereas, once we exclude Him, we use ourselves as leverage, causing us to play ourselves short eventually.

- ☐ We are asleep or sluggish when we should be awake on people, places, and things concerning our well-being, especially when it comes to our *Spirit to Spirit* Communion. When we have superfluous energy for the things of this world and zero energy for God, our Blueprinted Purpose, tending the Fruits of the Spirit, or developing Christlike Character, we will have issues from the inside out.

How can we counteract these actions? In all simplicity, give God what He wants, and He will grant us the desires of the heart.

Listen, He placed the desires within us, which means that He has the full details, regardless of how smart we think we are. Being that He knows them better than anyone, in the *Spiritual Vetting* process, it saves us precious time from jumping from one thing or person to the next, searching for what has already been Divinely Blueprinted or Predestined.

By all means, *'Playing Possum'* is not designed to point the finger. We will all experience such behavior at some point in our lives. Even children and small animals go through this phase without being taught, while at the same time having the most fun at doing so. If we deprive them of this process, we will cause them to become weak, vulnerable, and naive.

Frankly, it is in our nature to play these games with God, ourselves, and others, especially in our Egypt or Desert Experiences. Amid all, we are not designed to remain in such a state. It is for DEVELOPMENTAL PURPOSES ONLY, equipping us with the experiences needed to deal with or recognize the Vicissitudes of Life for this Heaven on Earth Experience and our Blueprinted Destiny.

In the same way that God Spiritually Anointed the Writers of the Bible to document Instructions or Revelations, He first TRAINED them thoroughly. And based upon their *Spirit to Spirit* Connection or Divine Encounters, it DOES NOT mean we must accept the Divine Wisdom left behind by our Forefathers as a Testament or Testimony. Spiritually Speaking, it is designed as a Grandfathered in, Spiritual Compass redirecting us toward the Promises of God without fail or reservation, but we must want it for ourselves, Spiritually Tilling our own ground.

To be clear, we DO NOT have to use the Divine Wisdom of the Word of God to become better, stronger, and wiser in Kingdom Formality. Why? It is a FREE WILL CHOICE to use, reject, or opt out, doing nothing. More importantly, whichever decision we make, we must be comfortable with it.

Why should we become comfortable with our decisions when exercising free will? They contain PROMISES! Therefore, let us take it to scripture before moving on. *"Behold, I set before you today a blessing and a curse: the blessing, if you obey the commandments of the LORD your God which I command you today; and the curse, if you do not obey the commandments of the LORD your God, but turn aside from the way which I command you today, to go after other gods which you have not known."* Deuteronomy 11:26-28. What does this mean in layman's terms? We determine our reality by our righteous or unrighteous decisions and behaviors, making it extremely important to know and understand the differences according to the Word of God, or doing things our way.

In properly examining ourselves, it behooves us to do this before committing to thoughts, actions, reactions, demeanors, biases, conditions, or words we do not understand or leading us into idolatrous efforts. I know it seems like it would take a lot of time. Once we become accustomed to conducting ourselves in such a manner, *As It Pleases God*, it becomes easier to decipher between righteous and unrighteous, good and bad, positive and negative, and so on, especially when MASTERING the Fruits of the Spirit.

By the same token, when embarking upon the Promises of God, we cannot say we do not have Divine Access, especially when we have the same Spiritual Connection to our Blueprinted Destiny as the next man, *As It Pleases God*. Simply put, if we desire to ACCESS the Promises of God, then we must ask ourselves what we are Spiritually Tilling for the Kingdom.

To say the least, if everything is about us, tilling for ourselves and no one else, then unfortunately, selfishness alone can deny the Spiritual Access needed to take us to the next level or *The Promises of God*.

Now, suppose we add a little disobedience, debauchery, pompousness, or hatefulness into the equation. In this case, we will find ourselves brewing up a mess and, sometimes, not realizing what we are doing because it has become our normal. Then again, certain things that we put ourselves and others through are unnecessary. Unfortunately, for some odd reason, we do it anyway, not realizing *The Promises of God* are attached to it, them, or that.

The Promises of God

As God Promised, He gave us the Holy Spirit to Divinely Cover us, and the Blood of Jesus as a formal sacrifice, granting us what we need to get us started on this Spiritual Journey from the inside out. But we rarely demand EXCELLENCE from ourselves, living by example for our up-and-coming Bloodline to carry the Mantle of Greatness. Yet, if we begin to approach life from a Spiritual Perspective in such a manner, the trajectory of our Blueprinted Mantles will definitely take on a life of their own. How is this possible, especially when we cannot control our lives or other people? Once again, this is where we are DECEIVED! We control what is taking place within us, spreading outwardly, making SELF-CONTROL extremely important.

Suppose we train our Bloodline to maintain and sustain a Positive Mindset, how to use the Word of God as a Spiritual Tool, maximize the Fruits of the Spirit, behave Christlike in any given situation, and become a work-in-progress toward their Divine Blueprint to gain Spiritual Leverage in the Kingdom, *As It Pleases God.* Do we think for a minute, God will allow our Bloodline to self-destruct when properly rooted and grounded in the Tree of Life? Absolutely not! He will prune what and who needs to be pruned, *As It Pleases Him,* for our sake. He did this for our Forefathers, and He will do it for us; we only need to Spiritually Position ourselves for Divine Greatness to intertwine itself the way God intended from the BEGINNING of time and according to the Gospels.

The Gospel in the Eye of God is the *Good News* we have been Divinely Predestined to receive with Supernatural Illumination, guiding us to the Light. Indeed, if we have not gotten the *'Hot Off The Press'* informative instructions by now, let me be the Spiritual Informant bringing the Divine Narratives on behalf of the Heavenly of Heavens.

First of all, the *Good News* is brought to and through us by the Blood of Jesus as our Formal Sacrifice, opening the Spiritual Doors of Revelation regarding the Promises of God. More importantly, second to none, it is also our Great Reward hidden in plain sight on how to Please God with a Cloak of Divine Wisdom, Secrets, Favor, and Mysteries of the Kingdom that is available to everyone but used by only a few.

How is it possible NOT to use our Great Rewards, especially when we are a Devout Believer, Blessed, and Highly Favored? I am not here to discount anyone's Spiritual Relationship with God; I am here to EXTRACT the Promises and Blueprints hidden within, maximizing our Greatest Potential in and out of the Kingdom.

In addition, I am also here to share pertinent information on how to Spiritually Capitalize on the Fruits of the Spirit while leading in the Spirit of Excellence and Christlike Character. What is the benefit of capitalizing in such a manner? Frankly, it guides us with a Spiritual Compass of Illumination, training us to use the Holy Spirit the way God intended. When used properly, in most cases, it catapults us into Divine Purpose, giving us the Unction to Function, *As It Pleases God* with Heavenly Provisions.

Listen, the Word of God is the Gospel we need to save ourselves, our Bloodline, and others through the vehicle of Divine Inspiration through Spiritual Principles, Beliefs, Laws, and Precepts documented by our Forefathers for a time such as this. Yet, the missing link to all of this is the Elements of Truth! More importantly, it is designed to *Spiritually Vet* out the Pharisees, Servants, Prophets, Disciples, and the wolves in sheep's clothing from the inside out.

What does *Spiritual Vetting* have to do with us? How we treat ourselves and others when no one is looking determines who we are from the inside out, even if we learn how to pretend, defend, or offend. Spiritual Examination has been around since the BEGINNING of time, and it is not going anywhere.

Why must we examine ourselves, especially when we are who we are? It allows us to lay the Gospel Truth on the table, causing us to sort through the known and unknown intricacies within the human psyche. How can we sort through what we do not know or understand? Fortunately, this is the reason for the Documented Gospels, guiding us through the life of Jesus while helping us understand ourselves through Kingdom Expectations and how to treat each other without judging or pointing the finger. Instead, offering Love, Compassion, Forgiveness, Mercy, Inspiration, and Hope in a positive demeanor, even if we are NOT benefiting in the matter through our natural eyes, yet operating in Kingdom Righteousness for Heaven's Sake.

The Unquenchable, Unquestionable, Unrelenting, and Unwavering Truth of our Heaven on Earth Experiences are here to Divinely Assist us on our Spiritual Journey without evicting us from being in Purpose on Purpose. Still, when yielding to our Divine Blueprint, we must allow it to do so without taking things into our own hands as if we can defy the reason for our being or boss God around, as if He is our puppet on a string. What does this mean, especially when God is for us? If we pay attention, when we attempt to force the Hand of God in unrighteous efforts, we secretly turn on ourselves without realizing it due to our amiss behaviors, thoughts, beliefs, or doubts.

Listen, no one is perfect, but intentionally using God in our debaucherous efforts creates Spiritual Violations, Taboos, and

Curses in the Realm of the Spirit. For this reason, we must tread with caution regarding what we lay at the Doorpost of God, especially when we know better and make a conscious effort NOT to do better!

How can we avoid entangling God in our Spiritual Violations? We should involve God in every aspect of our lives through the Holy Spirit, Repenting, Forgiving, Fasting, and Covering ourselves with the Blood of Jesus to self-correct before Spiritual Correction takes place. Is this NOT contradicting? Absolutely not! In the Kingdom, there is a BIG difference between INVOLVING God in our equational efforts of malice or PLACING Him at the forefront of our lives to build the Kingdom.

When USING God for selfish reasons, gains, manipulation, traumatization, or deception, tearing the Kingdom or His sheep down, we then have a problematic situation with Him. Hence, it behooves us to MASTER the intents of the heart, redirecting the 'Fix Me' concept to all of our ungodly, untamed, unfruitful, or counterproductive motives while regrafting them to righteous, positive, fruitful, and Godly.

The strategic, neatly woven Fabrics of the Gospel or Good News supersede the bad news of hidden trauma, setbacks, regret, or pain, especially if we open ourselves to positively learn from the experiences of others to become better, stronger, and wiser. To be clear, this does not mean we will not experience challenges or experience some form of thirst, hunger, or trauma. Actually, it means our challenges will not have us because we are Spiritually Equipped Mentally, Physically, and Emotionally with the Whole Armor of God, withstanding the wiles of the enemy. Approaching the Gospels in such a manner allows us to Learn, Grow, and Spiritually Till our own ground to SOW back into the Kingdom with our unique Testament or Testimony when the time is right or when called upon by the Heavenly of Heavens.

Divinely Possessing *The Promises of God* is the ultimate Spiritual Bliss most have yet to experience. Why do we not get to experience this as Believers? Most often, it is due to the lack of understanding, illumination, training, or inside information provided through the Gospels from God's Divine Perspective. To be clear, with all due respect, we are subjected to man's perspective of who God is or is not; however, we are not all the same.

We cannot place God in a box or on a rooftop, letting Him in when we feel like it, especially when He created it all, including man. More importantly, He is the ONE with the Final Authority, period! For this reason, we need the Holy Spirit involved to EXTRACT or CONVERT what is Divine, preventing the distortion of our Blueprinted Purpose. What does this mean in layman's terms? Euphorically, this is similar to processing diamonds or gold, changing into its revered state of valuable quality hidden within the layers of debris.

Objectively speaking, we all have something to work on in the Eye of God. In all transparency, it is best to have the Holy Trinity clean us up, allowing us to come forth as pure gold rather than pretending as if we do not need God's All-Knowing Eye, the Holy Spirit as a Comforter, or the Blood of Jesus as a Covering.

Is it possible to have it all together without God? Yes, we can have an illusion of having it all together by playing dirty, dabbling in idolatry, or going to the dark side, even if we reject the Heavenly Benefits associated. Please do not be deceived in this area: *"God makes His sun rise on the evil and on the good, and sends rain on the just and on the unjust."* Matthew 5:45.

Why are we advised to become Believers, especially when God rains on the just and unjust alike? It is a matter of choosing Kingdom Benefits over worldly ones, Divine Wisdom over worldly knowledge, Spiritual Eyes over worldly blindness, selflessness over selfishness, and so on. Yet, satiating ourselves in a worldly manner without God, when recompense comes seeking our names, we must ask ourselves, 'What or who will be the sacrifice for whatever or whomever?' Now, if we can live with our answer, then so be it! And, if we think this is not happening, then think again!

When the mask comes off, what will we do when we are exposed? When we are called out or brought to shame, then who are we going to call on? When our Bloodline has become a mirror image of our truth, is it fair to condemn them for the same things we are guilty of?

We can go word to word, toe to toe, vision to vision, or whatever to whatever, and we will not equate to our Heavenly Father or His Divine Word on our best day, regardless of how well we pretend to have it all together. Hence, it behooves us to step into *The Promises of God* to obtain what rightly belongs to us without playing hardball, constantly lying to ourselves or others, or pretending to be more than we are.

Why such bluntness in this matter, especially when we have the free will to do whatever, with whomever? From experience, when in the *Intensive Care Unit*, the hardball demeanor usually does not exist. When someone is genuinely fighting for their life, pompousness ceases unless there is an unrelenting demonic possession lingering within the human psyche. For the most part, being in such a state or on the brink of death comes with a form of humility that is already buried underneath our traumas or our something else. Still, it causes one to rethink how they are living or pray for a second chance to get it right in the Eye of God, *As It Pleases Him*.

Listen, and listen to me well. When we need what money cannot buy, it changes the most challenging person into a humble SERVANT in the Kingdom of God. In short, it behooves us to become Spiritually Proactive, including God in the equation of all things.

Why must we proactively include God, especially when we do not have it all together? No one has it together 100% of the time because we are all a work-in-progress with strengths and weaknesses, learning and growing daily. For this reason, we need the Holy Spirit to guide us continually. Plus, we need the Blood of Jesus to cover our known and unknown atrocities, keeping us Spiritually Synced in ONENESS with God. So, if we think we can approach the Vicissitudes, Cycles, and Seasons of life on our own without Spiritual Guidance from the Heavenly of Heavens, then have at it!

So, here we are with '*How To Please God*,' right? When the Kingdom of God is backing us, no man can contend or stop His Divine Promises. Moreover, they cannot circumvent the Gospels from unveiling what is veiled. Nor can they prevent our Divinely Blueprinted Purpose from doing what it is Spiritually Designed to do, *As It Pleases Him*.

Yet and still, if we do not KNOW or UNDERSTAND this Factual Truth for our Heaven on Earth Experiences, we can indeed miss our Spiritual Mark or Cue due to selfish or worldly deception, blindness, deafness, or muteness, causing us to second-guess what we ALREADY know. In any event, do not become alarmed when this happens. Why? It happens to us all due to our human frailties and normal brain fogs that cause us to forget things amid the Vicissitudes, Cycles, and Seasons of Life.

Amid all, our Spiritual Tools are available to Divinely Instruct us as we walk by faith and not by sight. Why do we need Spiritual Tools in this phase? When used correctly and *As It Pleases God*, they give us Spiritual Access to the Kingdom of Heaven on a level that will put our enemies and naysayers to boot.

Age of Faith

According to the Heavenly of Heavens, the *Age of Faith* or Spiritual Evolution is upon us, Building, Pruning, and Regrafting; therefore, we must step up our game, *As It Pleases*

God. Why must the things of God be a game? For example, if we play by the rules, we have a better chance of winning than cheating, right? Game or not, obeying or disobeying, this same concept applies in the Kingdom, and if we want Divine Grace to reside and abide within the human psyche, we must position ourselves to RECEIVE.

What is the purpose of being ready to receive from the Heavenly of Heavens? To ensure Divine Grace does not pass over whatever, with whomever, because the HEAVENLY CONSUMMATION is upon us, regardless of what we understand, believe, or deny.

In the past, God used the Prophets to speak to the masses, then He used His Son, Jesus Christ, and now He is speaking directly to us, *Spirit to Spirit*. How do we make this make sense in real-time? In the simplest form possible, He will speak directly to you in SPIRIT and TRUTH! Thus, you must selflessly position yourself to see, hear, understand, and speak CORRECTLY and *As It Pleases Him*.

When God is satisfied with us, He does not make it a secret. Without a doubt, He rewards us openly with no shame attached, GUARANTEED. Even if people think we are a little shaky, God has the Divine Power to balance us out. So, if you are ready to go to the next level of Divine Greatness, let us SEAL the DEAL and support the Movement of God.

With our *As It Pleases God*® Movement products, we extend a helping hand, leading the way into the Greatness you already possess under layers of something else. Nevertheless, the ultimate goal is to POUR into you Mentally, Physically, Emotionally, and Spiritually, enabling you to do likewise with another, activating the Law of Reciprocity. Many Blessings to All, and Grow Great.

Dr. Y. Bur

www.ingramcontent.com/pod-product-compliance
Lightning Source LLC
Chambersburg PA
CBHW071711160426
43195CB00012B/1650